Arcadian L.A.

and other essays

To Steve,

by Michael Jacob Rochlin

Michael Jacob Rochlin

Unreinforced
Masonry
Studio
Los Angeles

Typeset and printed in the United States of America
This book is printed on 100% recycled paper

Published by Unreinforced Masonry Studio
P.O. Box 33671
Los Angeles, CA 90033
(323)660-7092 or (888)875-2233 ext. 8767

Book Design by Hal Taylor
Cover Design by Randall Tinear
Anoakia drawings courtesy of Design Aid Architects
Historic Photographs from:
Photo Collection-Los Angeles Public Library
Photo-Collection-The Huntington Library, San Marino, California

Rochlin, Michael Jacob
Arcadian L.A.
ISBN# 0-9648304-8-5
Library of Congress #200309011
1. Architecture--California--LosAngeles.
2. History--California--Los Angeles Region.
Architecture-Los Angeles 3. Cities and Towns Planning--Los Angeles. I.Title.

1 2 3 4 5 06 05 04 03

To the memory of my father

Mercury's Magic Machine

In nowhere near the beginning, Biblical prose and classic imagery were mixed to booster 1880s boom land sales. A God-given cornucopia found and tamed by heroic Spanish, was handed down to the manifestly destined Yankee for him from which to feast. And later, water too, through an epically long siphon, fell from the hills for him from which to drink. And he cupped his hand and drank and drank.

Then when one day Cupid tarnished his tootsies in tar, oil was sucked from below and farms were divided into itsy-bitsy squares. The Spaniard's sword was recast as Thor's hammer and thrown to the mighty industrialist for him with which to mass-produce. And he mass-produced and mass-produced. And bungalows were built, and Mercury, the god of commerce, gave of his own helmet to be pounded into the form of a magic machine to fly from beach to river, valley to mountain. And the followers flew and flew, leaving but slow pokes to cry out for public space, social programs and housing.

Upon hearing these slow poke cries, the Gods raged, "Creeping Socialism!" And they devised a fearsome new plan accompanied by a strange and fantastic saga. It turned out that the city was separate from the land, real places to live were quite far, and it was best to use Mercury's magic machine to fly to work-a-day downtown, then back to bed, thy soles neither touching plain, canyon nor pass. And the city itself must "redevelop." Legal or no, the ding-ding, whirr-whirr streetcars must be dismantled; the city-center, cut off. Working-class suburbs must be severed, cut to pieces by new concrete ways that were "free." Die-hard density must be struck a lightning-thunder death blow, destroyed utterly, buried beneath stadiums, coliseums, arenas, convention centers and towers of business. Every house must be unto its own, independent of neighbors, dependent on corporate employers, informed by a magic story box. Progress! Work now and await the Olympian future.

Meanwhile in the great basin, eleven Main Streets begot a Miracle mile which begot shopping centers which begot regional malls. Palms towered high while troublesome questions shot through sidewalk cracks. Why is our air foul; our water bitter? Can not we make do with less, conserving our resources, cherishing our Mother Earth? Why now does our feast come from afar? Indeed, from the time of our forefathers, our county hast led the nation in harvests.[1] Must we spend so much time watching the magic story box and flying about in Mercury's machine?"

"Yes," came the answer for there is threat. "Evil empires may visit upon us fire and pestilence. Opium lords, communists, terrorists, rogues and tyrants gather at the city gates, devising our downfall. Banished are the rights you've fought for, the protections you've gleaned. You shalt listen to your magic story box. You shalt fly in your magic machine. How else will you guard your new concrete ways that are free?"

"But where shall we put our golden idols that we have earned--our punch bowls, Chippendales, picnic baskets and in-line roller skates?"

So the gods decreed, "Each shall have an ark--five by eight cubits. And it shall be called Self-Storage and it shall be quiet and controlled. And each sabbath, ye shall arrive in Mercury's magic machine and utter secret numerals so the citadel gate may slide and ye may enter the Kingdom and visit thy idols.

But heed, turn thy magic music talking box loud so as not to hear the chuga-chuga train with its fading whistle...for it is passed...and sad...and ye shall not bear it...for truly be it understood... thou too art like the train.

Woooo! Woooo!
Gush! Gush! Gush!
Zoooom! Hissss!
Beep! Beep!

*

1 "From 1910 to the early 1950s Los Angeles was the leading county in the nation in farm production." Leonard Pitt and Dale Pitt, *Los Angeles: A-Z* (Berkeley and Los Angeles, University of California Press, 1997) p. 6.

Fig. 1

Arcadian L.A.

With the vote freshly acquired, industrial, wildcat and jackpot fortunes in hand, and an early 20th century wide-reaching freedom of thought and action, affluent heiresses and wealthy widows found Southern California fertile ground for the evolution of their estates. Comfortably nesting their holdings in the majesty of the region's varied terrain, they combined art, architecture and landscaping to create enclaves that defined the expressive society of their time. [1] *They* devoted their adult lives to establishing, maintaining, and, in most cases delaying the demise of their ranch, farm, factory, hostelry, equestrian stable, cultural complex or social center homes. *We*, in the basin, valleys foothills and coast, live under the influence of their legacies.

Regionally, as a rule, expansive tracts were whittled down to small seats then individual

Fig. 2

Fig. 3

lots. Bitter struggles ensued when inheritors attempted to keep intact their bountiful bequests. A tale of landed beauties and business beasts, the setting for California's longest, greatest legal land battle was wind-blown Malibu beach. [2-3]

Once the southern end of the Coastal Chumash inhabitation,[1] a near 40,000 acre strip named for the villages Topanga, Malibu and Sequit, was ripped from native hands and granted, in 1804, to José Bartolomé Tapia, son of soldier recruit Felipe Santiago Tapia of Culiacán. Over the next hundred years, it passed through family lines and across several nationalities, until purchased by New Englander Frederick Hastings Rindge.[2] He died in 1905 at the age of forty-eight, leaving his 17,000 acre estate to his wife May.[3]

Continuing to raise crops and cattle, she built several homes, numerous outbuildings and dams, fought fires, conserved water, established and ran the well-known Malibu Potteries and watched her family grow.[4] Ironically, her main occupation became, however, simply keeping others (city, county, state and federal agencies, homesteaders, rustlers, returning veterans, thieves, engineers, water bandits and bootleggers) from encroaching upon her land. She established her own railroad as a legal maneuver to detour

Southern Pacific's tracks and also held off the state's Pacific Coast Highway for two decades.[5] As a respite, May stayed at her city home while her daughter summered at the Malibu Lagoon in a house designed by Stiles Clements.[6] Of May Rindge's extensive architectural efforts, for the public, that little fourteen-acre getaway is the principal remnant.

In the Spanish style, the Adamson House has cozy well-proportioned rooms, Moorish motifs and bright dramatic views from its subtly darkened interior. The house's bright accents are offset by the beach's blues and the garden's greens. [4-5] On all sides, patios have vaulted overhangs, turned wood screens, ornamental iron and carved wood benches with handcrafted nails. Inside, the living room's pointed Saracenic arch window looks out to the pier and Pacific.[7] [6] The dining room table offers a sea view from each seat, and the compact kitchen has a nook and toilet for the staff. The entry features a single turn stair case leading up to a skylit central foyer.

Upstairs bedrooms feature stone mantle fireplaces, decorative ceilings and polished wood floors. [7-8] Docents show off the space-saving folding table and the secret sliding panels. French doors open onto generous balconies while below in the court, grillwork ornaments

Fig. 4

Fig. 5

Fig. 6

Fig. 7

Fig. 8

the east elevation. A series of fountains lead to the Pool House where the blue plains of pool and sea imply Iberian indulgence—each dressing room an Andalusian farmhouse fantasy.[8] [9-11] This is an affluent American family retreat—a remnant of Southern California's coastal vacationing tradition.[9] Titillating tales are told: of the son's bachelor quarters,[10] of the daughters' giggling competition, of the father's nautical ambitions, of the mother's Spanish romanticism.[11] But it was none of these tid-bits that was to save the house from the bulldozers—it was the tile. [12-16]

A jade green seaweed-masked Neptune spits water into a coquillage tile bowl. Tile guardian peacocks adorn a Spanish Revival basin. Tile triangles radiate from the fireplace arch. Tile stars surface the patio tables. Tile circles tell time. Tile waves wash out from the wainscot. Tile mosaics cover the ledges. The east face may hint of the Alhambra but downstairs countertops are pure flag-waving Americana. Terracotta deck pavers might be found in a *Zorro* set while in the upstairs bathroom glazed hand-painted pirate ships sail across the shower wall. This is a Malibu Potteries showplace, a ceramics labor of love, a sand and sea rainbow of glazed clay.[12]

Fig. 9

Fig. 10

Fig. 11

Fig. 12

Fig. 13

Fig. 14

Fig. 15

Fig. 16

However scintillating, The Adamson House itself was but a dot on this twenty-five mile long ranch. After its completion, Mother Rindge began the fifty room "Castle" on Laudamus Hill. Unfortunately, as the project neared completion, at the height of the Depression, mounting construction costs, mounting legal fees and horseback mounted property patrols amounted to a final straw. To stave off bankruptcy, Rindge sold off plots that had previously only been leased. She let go a limited portion of the Malibu coast near Las Flores Canyon and finally dipped into her personal portfolio of stocks and bonds.[13] This proved insufficient, and after an involuntary petition of bankruptcy was filed she countered with her own petition holding off subdivision until 1940. A year later, nearly without funds, in her West Adams home, at the age of seventy-five, she died.

Newspapermen, cameras clicking in an intact wilderness, rather than recognizing the significance of her efforts, heralded a real estate open season. For them, with little mention of the preservation of miles of beaches and mountains, the reign of the defiant "Queen of the Malibu" had ended.[14]

On the other the end of those same majestic mountains, perhaps the best-known local heiress' estate was purchased in 1919 by Aline Barnsdall, daughter of oil-rich Pennsylvanian Theodore Barnsdall. Herself a somewhat successful Chicago producer, having inherited a substantial fortune, it was her intention to bring "Theater" out west. Envisioning a cast and curtain cultural community, she commissioned the nation's "most original" (and destined to be most famous) architect[15] to design the residences, offices, galleries, apartments, stages, waterfalls and winding entrance roads, of this thirty-six acre, olive-filled artist's Avalon. Within an ubiquitous grid, her U-shaped pinwheel of blocks house would be placed on the site's centerline with the proposed main theater on axis to the east. There would be fashion shows in the outdoor court, meetings over tea by the hearth, art shows in the gallery, picnics by the stream, a dramatic waterfall facing Vermont and shops, lofts and movies along *the* Boulevard. Each surrounding olive tree in this inclined grove[16] was to be either dashed for removal, or circled for ornamental attraction. The lush, natural orchard lanes would be given order by the "Master's" touch. Watercolor renderings would finally bring classic composition to slapstick prat-fall Hollywood banality.

Politically active, an art patron and all-in-all contrarian, Aline not only entertained

Margaret Anderson, Lawrence Langner, Emma Goldman, Norman Bel Geddes, Charlie Chaplin, D. H. Lawrence, George Bernard Shaw and H.G. Wells, she financially supported socialist Upton Sinclair for governor[17] and her campaign (donating funds, organizing events and lining her property with political billboards) to free imprisoned labor-leader Tom Mooney was critical to his release in 1939. She helped found the Hollywood Bowl, and eventually gifted her home and property to the Los Angeles City Department of Recreation and Parks.

It is, however, for none of this that she is most commonly remembered, but instead for a house in which she had but a short stay.[18] Named for her favorite flower, this house became...a thorn. With its Mayan ruin massing, its ornate and rhythmic capitals and cornice, its cantilevering overhangs, and its crown of the hill placement, the Hollyhock House was a powerful statement yes, but was it appropriate for willful Aline and five-year-old Sugar?

Inside, dimly-lit intermingling ochre and earth-tone Edwardian interiors (although somewhat softened by Japanese influence) conveyed a strange but still manly Chicago out west. Levels varied. Colonnades stretched down halls. Soffits lit the ceiling above. And did the bedroom have a bed? No, a Japanese futon stored away out of sight. The pre-designed furniture allowed for entertaining but not for more than six guests as "no more than six people can maintain intelligent conversation."[19] And will these six at least be able to relax back into comfortable chairs? No, they must sit straight, in fact, at ninety degrees. The walls were damp, the concrete door too heavy, the roof leaked badly.[20] Fort-like, Sugar's Nursery was heavy and hot. Sculptural rather than practical, the kennels resembled dominoes poised to tumble. [17-19] Formally, spatially, ornamentally, the Barnsdall buildings were the products of competing inventors, driven and destined to become the "Fantastic Four" of Southern California's Modern architectural elite—each one, fifty years later, internationally renowned.[21] A newcomer, socially ostracized, politically unpopular, manic, opinionated, the product of a broken home, her parents passed, a victim of vandals, a perpetually-pestered patron, and the subject of a 27-year FBI surveillance,[22] Aline, independent yes, yet still a novice mother and Angeleno, was most likely temporarily overwhelmed.

Conniving conservatives would have driven a more delicate constitution from town. Instead, routing both social and municipal rejection, she lived to see her estate established as a public park where in 1946, in Residence B, alone, she died.

Fig. 17

Fig. 18

Fig. 19

Meanwhile, hidden away in a drawer, near forgotten, was left behind a revolutionary vision arguably even more profound than her unusual house. Her undaunted persistence had, in the end, extracted the necessary know-how to give form to a dream. And that dream lay not so much in the field of theater nor residential architecture, but planning. During the "Master's" absence, she had nudged, coaxed, persuaded and pushed his son and two Viennese apprentices closer and closer to an L.A. land use general plan that was at least eighty years ahead of its time and...right on the money. [20-21]

Making positive use of available resources, her synthesizing vision:

- kept in place a large portion of the existing olive grove
- created commercial street frontage
- established a mixed-use border by placing residences above stores
- created a unifying central theme[23]
- established a social structure[24]
- limited and discouraged the overuse of the auto with a mere twenty-two parking spaces
- created a foundation for localized industry[25]

That was Barnsdall's model. A buzzing commune in the center of the city. Surrounded by orchards yet right on the street. In the field of Urban Planning, Olive Hill was the most

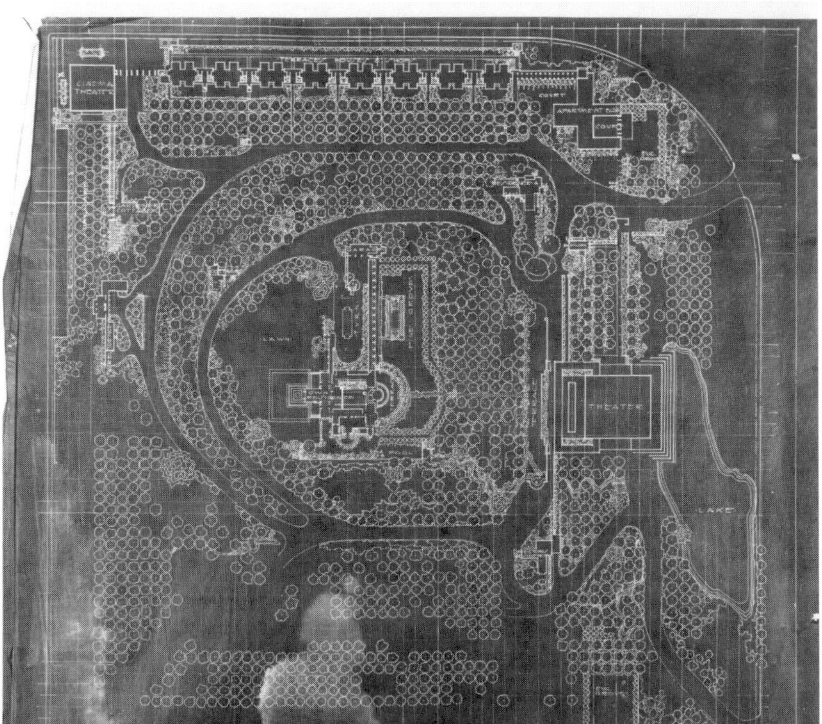
THEATER
LAWN
LAKE
COURT
GENERAL PLANTING PLAN
OLIVE HILL HOLLYWOOD CAL
FRANK LLOYD WRIGHT ARCHITECT

Fig. 20

BARN/STALL
THEATER
OLIVE
HILL

Fig. 21

far-sighted work of any of its legendary architects.[26] Its strength—the flexibility of its diagram. Whether adapted for Thespians, Athletes, Musicians or Nudists—it's central activity served to bind the residences, goods and services with a theme. *Ideally:* a monastery without doctrine, a university without red tape, an Olympic village without international pressure. *Plainly:* a quiet, calm campus with a calling.

How ironic that though the park bears her name, it is the haunting Hollyhock house which, at the beginning of the new millennium, is the obsessive focus of meticulous renovation. Witnessing its grounds reterraced, one wonders, upon reopening, will her contribution be remembered? [22-23]

Perhaps Aline foresaw this ambivalent conclusion for decades before the commencement of this renewal project, several years before her death, she wrote (ranted) to her famous employee of her disillusion. "I never felt right on Olive Hill...still on my quest for Arcadia in the U.S.A."[27]

Arcadia... Arcadia in the U.S.A. A lofty endeavor, yet for some, realized. Let's travel back to visit a truly Arcadian estate. An estate upon which oaks were once so beloved they were included in its very name.

Fig. 22

HOLLYHOCK HOUSE
Closed for renovation
Reopening April 2003

Fig. 23

Fig. 24

Fig. 25

Autumn 1999

Walking distance from the Los Angeles Arboretum, south of the shops and restaurants along Sierra Madre Boulevard is a forgotten nineteen-acre estate surrounded by thick concrete walls. Bordered by Foothill and Baldwin just north of the 210 Freeway, the grounds remain hidden behind locked steel gates. Over a dozen gray buildings sit amid nearly four hundred trees, a thick carpet of leaves fallen from their branches. Twisting oak limbs brush against a concrete architrave. By the Arcadia Wash, a sycamore throws its shadow over cement steps. Many of the trees predate the original owner—local heiress Anita Baldwin. Combining her first name and the name of the most prominent of these trees, she christened the headquarters of her six thousand acres "Anoakia." [24-26]

Now expensive cars, vans and trucks roll by outside, their drivers talking to people perhaps hundreds of miles away. The relentless drone of the 210 is punctuated on occasion by the calls of ravens, sparrows and blue jays. There are other animals here. Squirrels leap, lizards scurry, hummingbirds hum. A neighborhood cat pays a curious visit, gingerly exploring the empty tennis court, the abandoned music room, the dry swimming pool. The noisiest animals

Fig. 26

Fig. 27

Fig. 28

are a troop of wild parrots, most likely descendants of birds set free by Lucky Baldwin, Anita's father and founder of Arcadia. A portion of the once vast Baldwin Ranch is now the Los Angeles County Arboretum. The old Baldwin home is the hotel on the 70s television program, Fantasy Island. Anoakia itself has been used for location filming. Trash from the last production is scattered haphazardly throughout the site. A plastic soda bottle lays in the weeds, a potato chip bag is wadded up in a corner.

Each tree at Anoakia is marked with an aluminum tag. [27] Oak #39 twists and turns over its sheltered off-spring. Willow #346 appears more upright, forming a low to the ground "V". Beyond the trees a cluster of concrete columns lay scattered like a giant game of pick-up-sticks. [28] And beyond the columns, to the north, the solid San Gabriels meet the sky like a backdrop to a Western Movie. Where there are no leaves, little shoots of green sprout like fuzz on a peach. Weeds, reeds and flowering plants cover every column, every wall, every fence. Narrow bridges span the wash and picturesque roads gently curve around the buildings. Follow one road to the west end of the property to what appears to be the Parthenon—the Gymnasium. [29]

Fig. 29

Fig. 30

Shadows fall across a row of two-foot concrete pillars. Grass grows around the edge of their stepped base. A huge metal door squeaks open. Inside, there are high beams, engaged columns and clerestory windows. The building has not been used in years. Down a flight of stairs in the basement all that can be found are a stack of Civil Defense barrels for drinking water and tins of saltine crackers. [30] Returning outside though, the only army are ants methodically carrying away the remnants of a portico picnic. Acorns fall on the roof then roll along the slope collecting in the rain gutter. A Magpie carries a Guava twig in her beak. Will she nest atop the column capital or in the cornice rain spout? Maybe this season she'll choose the sill; maybe next, the projector room hatch.

Looking northwest, on the highest corner of the lot is Building 7--the worker's housing that became a dormitory. A recent horror movie filming has left it sooty, decrepit-looking. Down the other way is the farm building that became a preschool. [31-33] Pass through a long white picket fence and down three steps into its empty courtyard. There are broken green chalkboards and falling lights. There are cracked wooden cubby holes and faded Dutch trim. There are low benches and miniature club buildings, one like a Ranger's Station and the

Fig. 31

Fig. 32

Fig. 33

other like the Mikado's Palace. All that is missing are the high sing-song voices and the teacher's calm instructions.

Just on the other side of the wash, a two-foot deep bed of leaves lays under a huge oak. A variety of unusual trees surround the path. Could they be the same ones Anita Baldwin brought by train from the Panama Pacific Exhibition early last century?[28] Somewhere underneath this Autumnal carpet are the steps leading up to the pool. Dry leaves have taken the place of water, tan and rust shapes standing out against the sun-washed white tile. Inside, skylights illuminate the pool house lockers. Above the main room, there is a gaping hole. Scattered granite stones read: "Class of 1952", "Class of 1961", "Class of 1948." If not careful, it is easy to trip in the little square pond where Anita and the girls once cleaned their feet before breaking the sparkling liquid surface. [34-37]

Another hundred yards east is the Manor House. [38-64] A long arcade traverses the north side of this narrow mansion. Vines twist around columns and overgrown hedges block the walkways. Inside are three formal rooms, dining, drawing and library, equal in size and shape but different in treatment. Walls are paneled with fine woods; ceiling are coffered above window seats, fireplaces and glass displays.

Fig. 34

Fig. 35

Fig. 43

Fig. 37

Fig. 38

Fig. 39

Fig. 40

Fig. 41

Fig. 42

Fig. 43

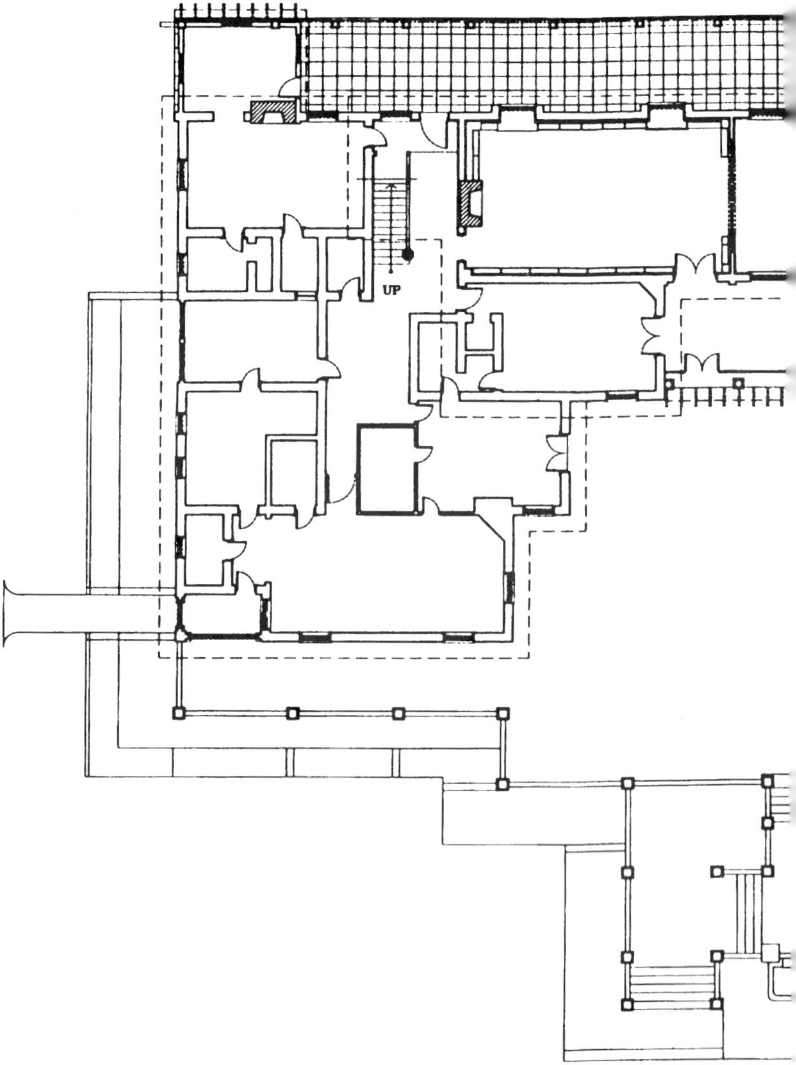

INTERPRETIVE FIRST FLOOR PLAN

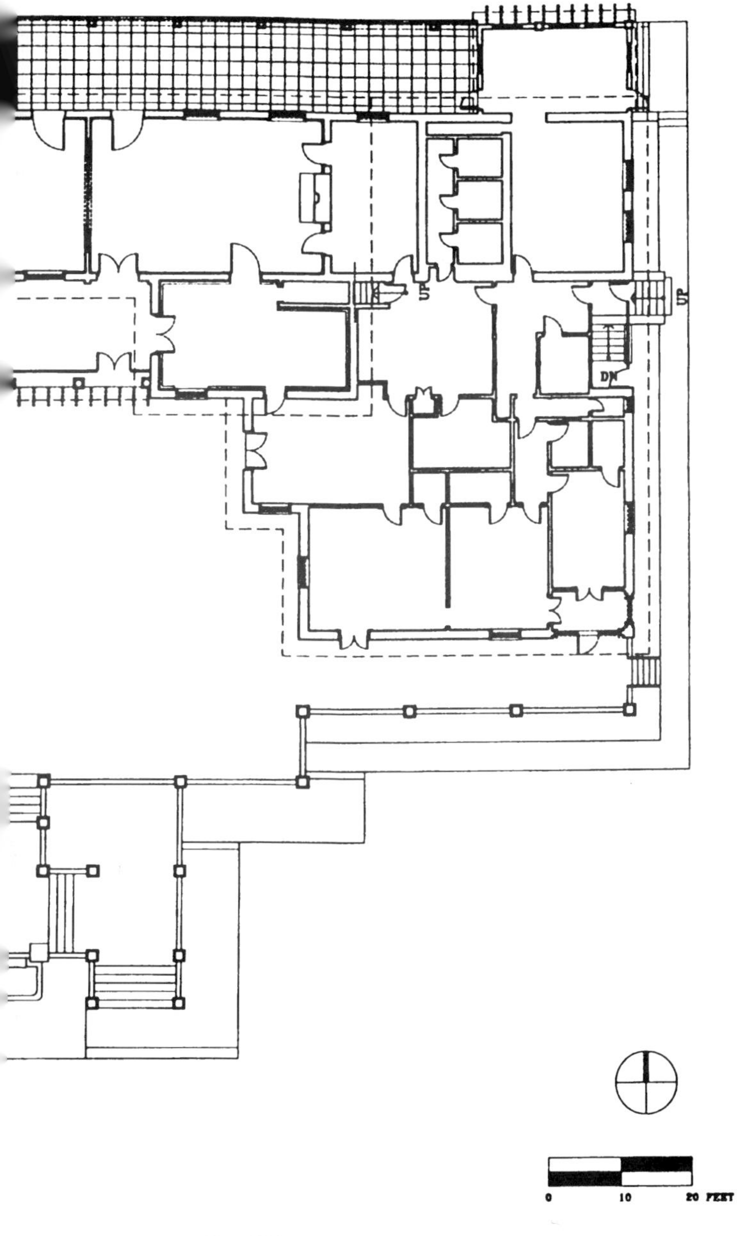

Fig. 44

Fig. 45

Fig. 46

Off the formal rooms a bathroom is furnished with a tub for two. A white tile kitchen holds three walk-in refrigerators. A loggia looks out to the garden. Upstairs the balcony has been enclosed. The paneled hall library has opaque French doors that separate the rooms. The hall leads to a sleeping porch at the end of which are steps to the roof.

Up there, the young San Gabriels loom large to the north and east. Tall and muscular, they cradle the low ground as they have for millions of years. For the last few thousands of those millions, people have inhabited the foothills and valleys. There have been at least four finds of Native American artifacts in the general area and what lies under these nineteen acres is still in question. The only artifacts on the roof though are discarded pieces of rope and scattered teardrop light bulbs. There are vents, skylights and eight chimney stacks. Bees buzz in and out of the attic. A dead mouse dries in the sun. Looking down on the wood chip paths of the front patio, it is easy to imagine groups of school girls taking their lunch break, sharing secrets, their long plaid skirts spread out like blankets. Here, they served punch during a school dance and clacked croquette clubs in summer.

A haze settles against the mountains and a cool breeze bends the branches of the trees.

Fig. 47

Fig. 48

Fig. 49

Fig. 50

Fig. 51

Fig. 52

Fig. 53

Fig. 54

Fig. 55

Fig. 56

Fig. 57

Fig. 58

Fig. 59

Fig. 60

Fig. 61

Traffic has gathered on the 210 freeway and like the white fly-crusted leaves on the mansion's hedge our city is being eaten away, fresh air replaced by fumes; gentle quiet, by the relentless hissing of rubber tires. Yet, inside these vine-covered walls the world remains composed. A tree grows from the center of the hedge circle, the pergola catches the sun. It is balmy, peaceful. Although the bees may not agree, for people, life is not so hurried, time, not so important, age, a blessing instead of a curse.

Return to the ground floor. The photographers and the armed guard have gathered at the top of the basement stairs. Exchanging ghost stories they speculate what could have set off the basement alarm. The electricity has been turned off. Silver-plated pistol drawn, the guard descends to the foot then scurries back up. Down there, all is dark except for the den, light penetrating the bottle-bottom windows and filling the space with an underwater glow. In the blackness, only the cat sees, exploring the different rooms, storage and utility spaces. She passes through the Indian motif folding doors and down the long bowling alley. Smelling the fermentation, she comes to the wine cellar and climbs the eight-foot high, hundred-year-old cask. Meanwhile outside, it has begun to rain. Quickly, visit one more

Fig. 62

Fig. 63

Fig. 64

Fig. 65

building—the Stables. [65-68]

Anita Baldwin was not only a philanthropist, humanitarian and art patron, she was also an avid animal lover tending and nurturing Anoakia for over twenty-five years. Dogs barked in the kennels, birds chirped in the aviary, bees buzzed in the apiary, and in the stables, thoroughbred horses neighed and whinnied in anticipation of a drink from the courtyard trough. Later when the grounds became the "Flintridge School for Girls," classrooms took the place of the stables and some of the over one hundred students bounded up to their dorms. From there, they gazed out at the oak growing through the roof near the front wall. What filled their minds in this mysteriously beautiful school setting?

Now, rain is coming down in earnest. Washing away the dust, the drops turn the light gray walls dark. As the wind whistles, acorns mush underfoot and the animals hide from the storm—it is time for us leave Anoakia.

Once back out on Baldwin Avenue, the metal gate swings shut, once again chained and locked. [69]

Fig. 66

Fig. 67

Fig. 68

SOUTH ELEVATION

Fig. 69

Spring 2000

Now Autumn and Winter have passed. It is Spring. The white and lavender wisteria, the pink and red camellias, the yellow daisies, the bright orange Birds of Paradise, the purple Irises, are all abloom amidst the rusted iron work, cracked enamel and peeling paint. [70-71] The mulberries are budding green and the scent of orange blossom floats. But Spring has also brought strange changes. The mansion has been striped of its ornament; tall white power poles erected by the walls; large red X's spray painted on the trees. Why is Anoakia being prepared for demolition? [72-75]

Whether viewing photographic exhibits in a courtroom or even surveying a site in person, many have difficulty seeing significance--historic or aesthetic. Anoakia—its buildings, its design, its landscape—embodies a way of life, an appreciation of different cultures, a relationship to nature—sun, water, air, ground, trees, animals, hills. Buttressed concrete walls line the street and within their boundaries a tender spirit reigns. [76-80] The Manor's arcades, pergolas and orientations unify the outside with the in. The Bathhouse aligns with the creek celebrating a love of water. Animals—horses, dogs and birds—were once cared for at the northern end

Fig. 70

Fig. 71

Fig. 72

Fig. 73

Fig. 74

Fig. 75

Fig. 76

Fig. 77

Fig. 78

Fig. 79

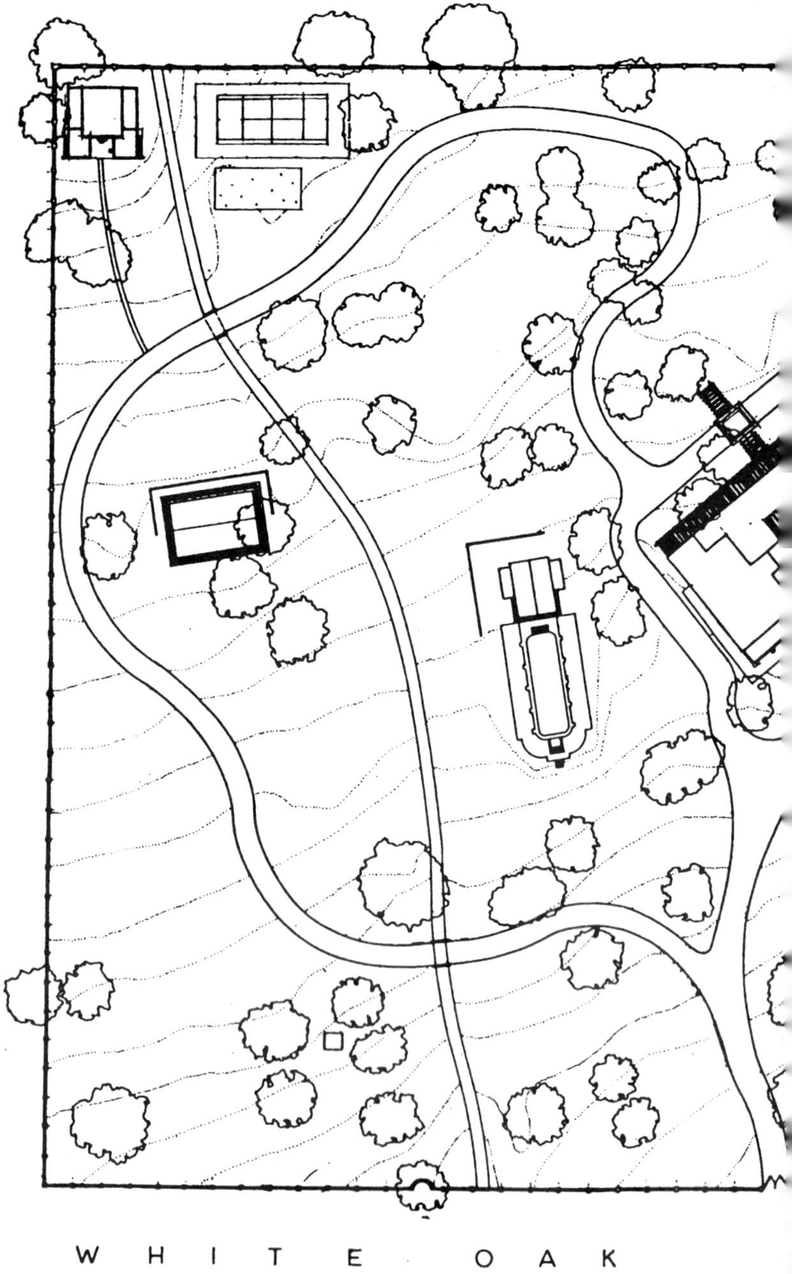
W H I T E O A K

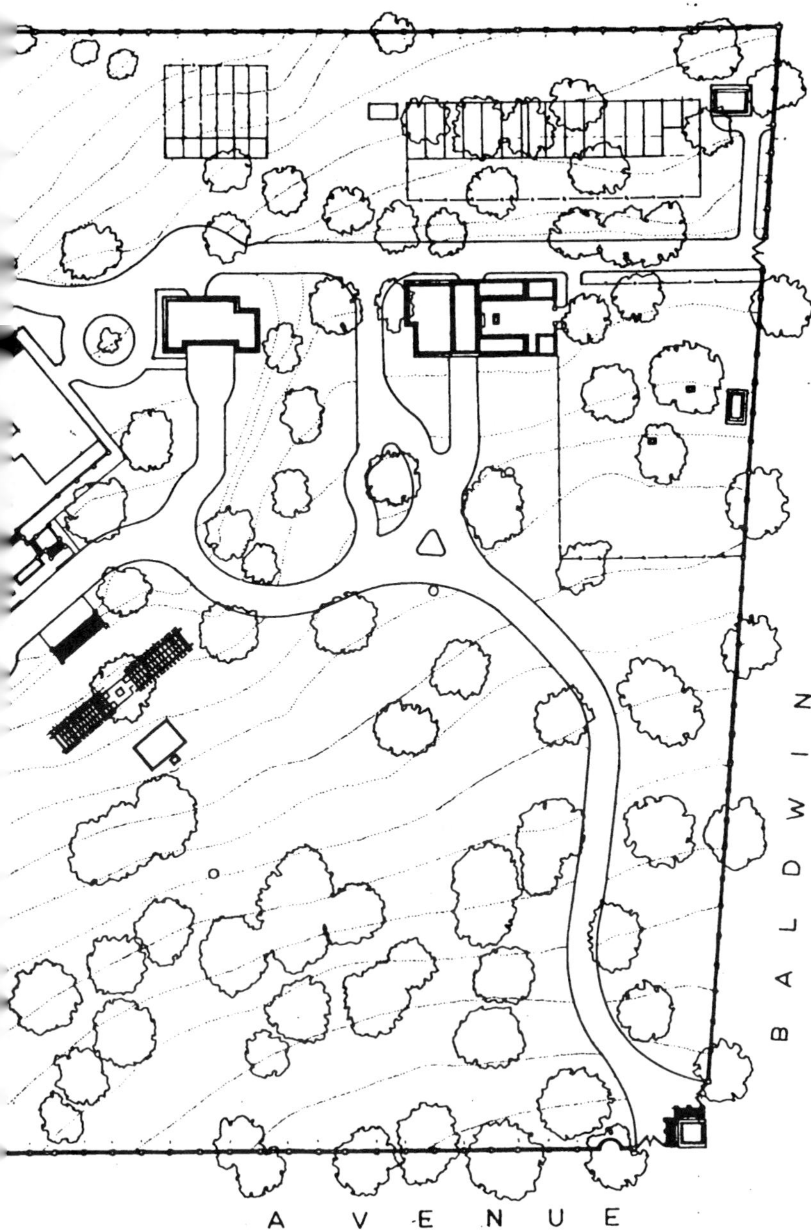

Fig. 80

of the site where the mountainous background is most present. The earth's gentle slopes were respected, not terraced. Oaks throughout the site were not chopped down, but encouraged to grow and reproduce, roads and buildings constructed around them. [81-82] The Italian Renaissance and Classic Greek styles reflect early 20th Century fashion, but the more plain Mission Revival elements of the other buildings, together with the overall site plan represent a thoughtful response to the natural conditions of the land as well as an acknowledgment of the many different peoples who have inhabited it. During a time of intense overconsumption and environmental destruction, Anoakia is especially significant--a softer touch, a less violent relationship to our surroundings.

Summer 2000

A local community group is trying to save Anoakia. They attend city council meetings and have obtained a prominent lawyer. Unfortunately, appeals to halt demolition are denied. A press conference is held and covered by a local station. A well-groomed reporter interviews members of the community group and films the site. The report is not shown because of coverage of a car chase.[29] All buildings are torn down but the mansion which is stripped of its artifacts.[30]

Fig. 81

Fig. 82

Fig. 83

Fig. 84

All that remains now of Anoakia is the (gateless) Gate House, [83] the (filled-in) wall and the (reoriented) bronze relief. The manor is gone; most trees, missing; the land, cut and regraded. On the thirty-one tiny plots multi-million dollar homes with Styrofoam cornices and thin rock veneers line "Anita Avenue" and "Horse Carriage Lane." [84-85] By the entrance, where the concrete once considerately veered around an old Oak, the niche remains but the tree has been removed. The old concrete pergola was discarded, replaced by a new wood one painted white for the gated community grand opening. Before, ground cover absorbed water, feeding it down to thirsty roots. Now plastic pipes drain it to of all places—the ocean, polluting Long Beach harbor with erosion, debris and runoff chemicals. [86-87]

A tragic, senseless loss? Clearly. Yet equally as clear, the predominate pattern of the last one hundred years. Here, in Southern California, places like Malibu Lagoon State Park and Olive Hill are rare exceptions, Anoakia is the rule.

Yes here in Southern California, where canoes cut choppy waters and May Rindge's

Fig. 85

Fig. 86

Fig. 87

Fig. 88

resolve upheld nature's beauty against winds of change; here, where bitter fruit were cured and Aline Barnsdall harvested a blueprint boulevard corner collective; here, here in this Arcadia, "simple and innocent, peaceful and pastoral," "where natives bear gifts, cattle graze and shepherds dream," where Anita Baldwin, synthesizing nature and architecture, running her award-winning farm, emulating her flamboyant father's avocations--dogs, hogs, steer, stallions, vine and wine. Here...here on an oak-filled estate, as throughout the county, the grounds were gouged, having remained privately owned, into speculative grasp, fallen.[31] [88]

***

1 Chester King, *Native American Indian Cultural Sites in the Santa Monica Mountains* (Topanga, California: Santa Monica Mountains and Seashore Foundation, 2000) pp. 52-56. Many coastal and inland villages were once located on what was to become the Rindge Ranch. "The wide range of marriage ties to both Santa Monica mountains Chumash and Western Tongva settlements appears to reflect the central place of Humaliwo in the political organization of the Western Tongva and Santa Monica Mountains Chumash."

2 Tapia's heirs sold Rancho Malibu to in-law Leon Victor Prudhomme who sold it to Matthew Keller. Keller received a patent for 13,316 acres from the U.S. Government who declared the remainder (excepting some homesteaded terrain) there's. Keller sold the land

to Rindge who added approximately 4,000 acres writing a contented memoir in the process. See Randolph Jorgen, *Mountains to Ocean-A guide to the Santa Monica Mountains National Recreation Area* (Tucson: Southwest Parks and Monuments Association, 1995) pp. 48-49. Also, Frederick Hastings Rindge, *Happy Days In Southern California* (Cambridge and Los Angeles, 1898).

3 May was eight years younger than her husband. W.W. Robinson, *The Malibu* (Los Angeles: Ward Ritchie Press, 1958), p. 22. Also see Leonard Pitt and Dale Pitt, *Los Angeles: A-Z* (Berkeley and Los Angeles, University of California Press, 1997) pp. 420 and 434.

4 On a Malibu Canyon site, Frederick Rindge named "Laudamus Hill," a Victorian mansion was built which burned in a 1903 firestorm. At this same site in 1929, May Rindge began construction on a 50-room Morgan, Walls and Clements-designed Mediterranean mansion. Declaring bankruptcy in 1936, she was never to finish nor occupy "The Castle," which was sold together with 26 acres of land to the Franciscan Order for $50,000 to become the Serra Monastic Retreat. May Rindge also raised other livestock including 400 pigs that disappeared near Zuma Canyon over a two month period. W.W. Robinson, *The Malibu* (Los Angeles: Ward Ritchie Press, 1958), pp. 32 and 37. Also, Marcia Page, Editor, *Ceramic Art of the Malibu Potteries* (Malibu: The Malibu Lagoon Museum, 1988), pp. 106-111.

5 As owner of the Hueneme and Malibu and Port Railroad, May Rindge was the only railroad owner of her gender in the nation. The Southern Pacific route was detoured through the Santa Susana Pass in observance of a law that landowners did not have to submit to two railroads passing through their property.

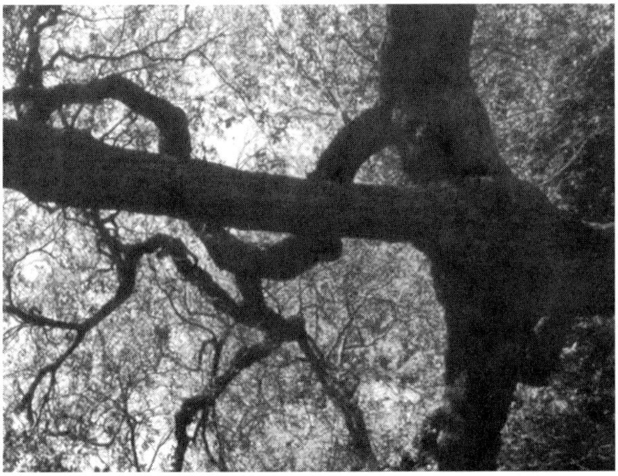

Pacific Coast Highway finally did go through in 1928. W.W. Robinson, *The Malibu* (Los Angeles: Ward Ritchie Press, 1958), pp. 31-34

6 May's home was in the Adams District, once the city's preeminent residential areas. The Adamson beach house was one of Stiles Clements' few residential commissions. David Gebhard and Robert Winter, *Los Angeles-An Architectural Guide* (Salt Lake City: Gibbs Smith, 1994), p. 6. May Rindge's daughter Rhoda married Merritt Huntley Adamson. They had established Adohr Dairy (Adohr is Rhoda backwards) in 1916. Marcia Page, Editor, *Ceramic Art of the Malibu Potteries* (Malibu: The Malibu Lagoon Museum, 1988), pg. 94. Also, Greg Hise and William Deverell, *Eden by Design-The 1930 Olmsted-Bartholomew Plan for the Los Angeles Region* (Los Angeles: U.C. Press, 2000), p. 17.

7 Fifty-foot openings like these appeared in the Mosque of Ibn Tooloon (built 879 A.D.) in Cairo. The arch was used as a symbol of the faith either formed of two segments of a circle, or, as a four-centered arch. The pointed arch was employed as early as 722 B.C. in the drains under the Great Palace at Khorsabad. Sir Banister Fletcher, *A History of Architecture on the Comparative Method* (London: B.T. Batsford, Ltd., 1921) pp. 47 and 834-838.

8 As the Malibu Lagoon State Beach's main source of maintenance income is weddings, the Pool House dressing rooms are reserved for brides and maids. At present there is an on-going battle between park maintenance and historic preservation.

9 Naples to Venice, Long Beach to Redondo Beach, Santa Monica to Santa Barbara, by the late 19th century, the tradition of wintering, recovering or staying the

summer on the California coast was well established. See Kevin Starr, *Material Dreams-Southern California Through the 1920s* (New York: Oxford University Press, 1990) pp. 246-250. Also see Leonard Pitt and Dale Pitt, *Los Angeles: A-Z* (Berkeley and Los Angeles, University of California Press, 1997) pp.259-261, 426-427, 454-455.

10 Now the Gift Shop.

11 The out buildings hint at diversion rather than necessity. The chicken coop was in the middle of a sand dune; the apiary, by the work room. The lath greenhouse and men's and women's dressing rooms bespeak not of ranching but of vacationing--a Spanish-style summer get-away profusely set with colorful tile.

12 Malibu Potteries produced a line of tiles from 1924-6-1932 which can be found throughout Southern California homes and institutions. Marcia Page, Editor, *Ceramic Art of the Malibu Potteries* (Malibu: The Malibu Lagoon Museum, 1988)

13 Her portfolio brought in approximately one million dollars (about a quarter of its value). The leased then later sold lots included the famous Malibu Movie Colony. W.W. Robinson, *The Malibu* (Los Angeles: Ward Ritchie Press, 1958), pp. 36-38.

14 March 6, 1936 headlines read, "Queen of the Malibu Fights For Her Fortune." Like Leonis, dubbed "King of Calabasas," local large land owners were given mock journalistic royalty. Rindge was portrayed as keeping the public from its coast. Ironically, though even the 1930 Olmstead Bartholomew plan for the L.A. region expresses a desire to obtain the beaches for the "people," it was May Rindge who later hired Olmstead after the Chamber of Commerce purposely and permanently shelved their report.

15 By this time Barnsdall had been working with FLW for several years. Wright, at a difficult point in his career, was to receive from Barnsdall during the years 1914 to 1924, forty-five commissions. Kathryn Smith, *Frank Lloyd Wright, Hollyhock House and Olive Hill-Buildings and Projects for Aline Barnsdall* (New York: Rizzoli, 1992), pg. 20. Also see, Meryle Secrest, *Frank Lloyd Wright-A Biography* (Chicago: University of Chicago Press, 1992) pp. 265-270.

16 Once just a part of Los Angeles' agricultural wealth--the county's primary income in the 19th century and a significant factor in the 20th. Incredibly, from 1910 to the early 50s, L.A. led the nation in farm production. Leonard Pitt and Dale Pitt, *Los Angeles: A-Z* (Berkeley and Los Angeles, University of California Press, 1997) pp. 6-7.

17 Norman M. and Dorothy K. Karasick, *The Oilman's Daughter-Biography of Aline Barnsdall* (Encino: Carlston Publishing, Inc., 1993), pp. 165-170.

18 According to Norman M. and Dorothy K. Karasick, *The Oilman's Daughter-Biography of Aline Barnsdall* (Encino: Carlston Publishing, Inc., 1993) pp. 88, "Aline was relieved to rid herself of Hollyhock House. It was never meant to be a home." Kathryn Smith, *Frank Lloyd Wright, Hollyhock House and Olive Hill-Buildings and Projects for Aline Barnsdall* (New York: Rizzoli, 1992) pp. 160-161, quotes Barnsdall about Hollyhock House directly, "Its ornate beauty never satisfied me." According to Charles Moore, *Los Angeles-The City Observed* (New York: Vintage Books, 1984), p. 253, "...she moved out of her house three years after it was completed." This is possible, however, she did not move in immediately after its opening and spent much time traveling. Her occupancy, by most all accounts was tentative and unenthusiastic. She preferred Residence B.

19 Norman M. and Dorothy K. Karasick, *The Oilman's Daughter-Biography of Aline Barnsdall* (Encino: Carlston Publishing, Inc., 1993) pp. 77-78.
20 Kathryn Smith, *Frank Lloyd Wright, Hollyhock House and Olive Hill-Buildings and Projects for Aline Barnsdall* (New York: Rizzoli, 1992) p. 161.
21 Frank Lloyd Wright, Lloyd Wright, Richard Neutra and Rudolph Schindler.
22 Norman M. and Dorothy K. Karasick, *The Oilman's Daughter-Biography of Aline Barnsdall* (Encino: Carlston Publishing, Inc., 1993) pp. 77-78.
23 In this case related to the region unlike the misplaced themes of many recent malls.
24 A hierarchy.
25 Not only commercial theater but all the associated craftwork. With stores keeping goods and services at hand, trips are reduced, conserving energy. Eventually, the idea of resuming harvesting olives for profit may have created an additional source of income for the fledgling commune.
26 Broadacre City for Los Angeles would have been a zoning and environmental nightmare. Uniform, auto-dependent and exaggerated, it suffered from numerous misguided Modern planning tenets. The communal housing exercises of Lloyd Wright, Richard Neutra and Rudolph Schindler featured cars in every garage and more frequently shared paths rather than meeting space or gardens. With all their drive, it was only with Barnsdall's willful restraint that a diagram as viable as Olive Hill—a model for Los Angeles central city planning--evolved.
27 This particular letter (Barnsdall to Wright, August 9, 1943) was a two-page typed tirade from which not even George Gershwin escaped.

28 Historic Building Report Design Aid by Portia Lee. Drawing of Manor Floor plan by Henry Ramirez. Drawing of Gate House by Kathleen Cooper. Drawing of Site Plan by Michael Jacob Rochlin. Site Model by Michael Jacob Rochlin and Tateshi Nagamine.
29 The coverage of the Anoakia protest was shown the following day.
30 Thirty-one homes are to be built on these nineteen acres significant not only for Baldwin's contribution but as a probable Native American site. Several prominent historians agree that it is likely Native American and other historically significant artifacts will be unearthed during construction. Though its Environmental Impact Report prohibits discarding unearthed artifacts, it is highly unlikely any will be reported as found--a common developer practice.
31 Arcadia City Council members Roger Harbicht, Roger Chandler and Gino Roncelli all voted to allow demolition and construction to proceed. Orange County Developer Arcadia Oaks L.L.C. (Mark Smith) after having purchased the property for approximately fifteen million dollars has already built many of the planned thirty-one homes.

Fig. 98

Fig. 1

Basin Invocation

In a desperate attempt to bridge the harsh divide between new and old, high and low, Modern and Beaux Arts, sterile and ornate, downtown developers ordered their design wizards to conjure imagery of Florence, Italy. Not a bad distraction, for *A Firenze, gli occi guidano, i piedi seguono.* From palace to piazza, statue to square--a spontaneous tour--no map needed; no guide required. In the walled city's center, the cathedral dome, *Il Duomo* is directly connected to two important public spaces. Approaching *Piazza della Signoria*, the *Pallazo Vecchio* towers above, luring visitors towards the *Loggia de Lanza.* From there, they are irresistibly drawn down the Uffizi Gallery to the Arno River and across the medieval *Ponte Vecchio.* Hours later, these same tourists arrive back on the dome's opposite side where in the *Piazza della Santissima Annunziata,* several buildings over time, have been made to compliment one another, sacrificing self-expression for the sake of the square.

Back home, though our own public space House Antipasto Platter is more a Leprechaun Lodge Hodge-Podge, at least the downtown public library's south entrance is well done. [1]

Fig. 2

As the terminus to Hope Street, its axis (leading through to the foyer) is fulfilled. Marching up, several flights of steps are crossed by a path leading west to the gardens; east, to our most established hotel. The facade is nicely preserved. A row of plynths personify categories of knowledge. “Statecraft” bears a severe, almost cruel expression. “Astronomy,” seemingly overwhelmed by the eclectic range of surrounding styles, stares out away from the highrise grid. “History” grasps a stone staff. “Letters” grips a petrified pen. “Arts” pinches a chiseled paint brush while “Science” holds a palm of stone stars. [2] Though as a bunch, they appear less than blissful, library patrons--biking, reading, writing, resting, romancing--appreciate this Cypress[1] and Bird of Paradise-filled transition zone--downtown's best-planned public space. [3]

Meanwhile, less than a mile northeast, on the other side of the 101, just below Olvera, [4-6] the Temporary Contemporary is another interesting example. Adaptive reuse (transformed in 1982 from a patrol car maintenance warehouse to office and exhibition space), it led the way for similar adjacent renovations. Initially intended as a brief substitute, it is now the center of a cultural complex. [7-10]

Fig. 3

OLVERITAS VILLAGE
UPSTAIRS
W-24
W-24
UPSTAIRS
W - 24
OLVERITA'S

Fig. 4

Fig. 5

Fig. 6

Fig. 7

Fig. 8

Fig. 9

Fig. 10

The library and the museum as if resting in a sculpted hand are among L.A.'s precarious urban stars. For the larger part, throughout the county, our plazas, paths, playgrounds, parks and preserves, cut off by cars, roaring roads, ubiquitous billboards and ceaseless traffic, are less able to engage. Without intercommunication, these drifting ships remain disconnected. Though we might aspire to emulate Florence, Chicago or New York, a connected city remains for us, an elusive goal.[2] More often, symbolic, artistic and municipal gestures reach for the identity of our city and its relation to public space. One such gesture, [11] a "list" of L.A.'s most familiar spots, can be found on our city's west side.

Most have come to expect weekend crowds milling about the quaint remnants—bottle-bottom windows, brick arch patios, tile benches and brass lanterns—of Westwood Village's high society past. [12-17] Strolling Weyburn Avenue, however, tourists may be surprised to bump into a pair of three-foot tall cement dice. And down, beneath their feet are Monopoly-style sidewalk inlays: "Farmer's Market," "The Music Center," "Sunset Boulevard." Shall we buy? If only it were that simple. "Chance" may send us to a Marvin Gardens of roses, a Boardwalk by the Pacific, a Reading Railroad in minature or a jail of vying jurisdictions, inadequate facilities and inaccessible sites. Advancing after doubles, the thimble asks

Fig. 11

Fig. 12

Fig. 13

Fig. 14

Fig. 15

Fig. 16

Fig. 17

itself: have I landed in a City, County, State, Federal, private, corporate or institutional square?[3] [18] Am I in a monument, a mall or a movie?

Monopoly's early thirties origins are contemporary to Westwood's initial opening. And the district's architect, St. Louis' Harland Bartholomew, was no stranger to city planning.[4]

Driving up into the empty rolling hills with the Janss Investment Company, what was once native[5] was to become European. [19] Not only houses and hotels but boulevards and boutiques, cafes and courts, pergola trellises and pinnacle towers. Execution: make it Mediterranean, write off the hills to the UC regents,[6] and move in the movies. Who would have dreamed college attendance would reach 35,000,[7] highrises would line Wilshire, billions of cars would commute through Sepulveda Pass and the Federal Cemetery would fill after an unending string of wars. [20-23] Once a Latin-style villa between downtown and the ocean, now a low-scale hold out—West L.A.'s public space veteran.

And where did all the returning soldiers go? As our bus has finally arrived, suffice to say, not into mass rapid transit. But lets leave that discussion for other days and leave the credit cards and colored concrete for other soles. For now, we climb aboard the Wilshire eastbound to an indigenous natural resource and the largest known trap of prehistoric animals. [24]

Fig. 18

Fig. 19

Fig. 20

Fig. 21

Fig. 22

Fig. 23

Fig. 24

Fig. 25

Better known by the redundant name La Brea Tar Pits, Hancock Park is an archaeological landmark, an historic monument and the home of two prominent museums. [25] With winding paths, amphitheaters and a picturesque stream, unlike Point Fermin or Rancho Los Encinos, Hancock is a county park favored by performers luxuriating in LAPD's lack of jurisdiction.

Taken from the Indians and granted to Antonio Rocha in 1828, "Rancho La Brea," thirty-two years later was purchased by Major Henry Hancock, who tapped it for its crude oil then sold it off to other elites. Large bones were often found and in 1906 a UC professor guessed of the pit's pleisocenic secret. Donated to the county in 1916, the park remained fairly isolated [26] until the twenties when department stores began to appear along Wilshire.[8] By the forties, the over one hundred upscale retail shops of the "Miracle Mile" served as focus for surrounding residents (gradually fading over the following twenty years, losing trade to suburban malls).

It was then in 1965, after an administrative split, that the Los Angeles County Museum of Art was moved from Exposition to Hancock Park. [27-33] The initial complex of buildings was set on a podium. Surrounded by a moat, the accompanying seepage of tar and water made it seem as though the site was resisting intrusion.

Fig. 26

Fig. 27

Fig. 28

Fig. 29

Fig. 30

Fig. 31

Even so, in 1976, the Page Museum opened housing exhumed skeletons and educational exhibits. Then, in 1982 a Post-Modern style addition altered the existing relationship between grounds and museum, taking it out to the street with a large scale entrance and atrium. Six years later, an contextless addition[9] further encroached on the park coming to within feet of the Tar Lake. Finally in the late 90s the old May Company and its parking lot were incorporated, renovated and together with the park, collectively cohered by careful landscaping and an attractive fence. This twelve million dollar improvement served to help reestablish an identity for the overbuilt site.[10]

Balancing better the boundaries with the buildings, now there are curving paths, green meadows, native shrubs and outdoor theater. Cactus flowers bloom. Bag pipes blow. Banjoes boom. Brutus backstabs. After an afternoon of Georgia O'Keefe and Salvador Dali, Incan effigies and Mayan marvels, Romanesque altars and Gothic tombs, breathe in the primordial scent of tar in this bubbling and beautifully eerie atmosphere.

Later, back on the bus, gradually realizing that not only is time relative, but size as well, we meander past Beverly Center, P.D.C.'s Blue Whale, [34-35] Farmer's Market, Park La Brea

Fig. 32

Fig. 33

ONES

Fig. 34

Fig. 35

and the Cinerama Dome [36] to the biker helmet shop [37] on our city's most wild and wooly way.

Hollywood Boulevard, more than Wilshire, Sunset, Santa Monica, Venice, Imperial, Olympic, Adams, Washington, Pico, Manchester, Slauson...is easily imagined as public space--its reputation for high and low budget expression working well with its orientation dividing glamorous hills and industrious flats. At night, lights impress. During the day, however, residents run ordinary errands while tourists stare down at their feet. Why? Let's go back over two hundred years and see if we can find out.

Where the ultra-modern concrete benches of Hollywood Franklin Park now sit is approximately where the Portola expedition encountered native peoples to whom the land was home. Later, after their home was stolen, and, Ranchos La Brea and Feliz had passed through many a hand, Hollywood was platted out in 1887. Methodist Kansans Horace and Daeida Wilcox established a dry town, offering free lots to any who would build a church.[11] In 1910 with a population of 4,000, Hollywood was consolidated with Los Angeles and by 1920, its main Boulevard held over 200 stores.[12] It was then, with the influx of movie makers, department stores, specialty boutiques, variety shops, showrooms and restaurants that the town became a competing retail corridor to Broadway. [38-44] The industrious flats assured an influx of goods, services and customers while the hilly back-

Fig. 36

Fig. 37

Fig. 38

Fig. 39

Fig. 40

Fig. 41

Fig. 42

Fig. 43

Fig. 44

Fig. 45

drop and eclectic buildings kept the romantic imagination in place.

By 1930 there were some 300 stores along the heart of the Boulevard and another 100 on the side streets.[13] The 40s continued the mystique with canteens providing an imaginary hometown to GIs. After the HUAC Red Scare of the 50s had initiated a period of decline, the Walk of Fame was begun as a street improvement. In 1986 an area from Gower to La Brea was designated an historic district and Metro stops opened in the 90s. This set off an unbalanced tug of war between preservation and large scale development. Caught in the middle, Hollywood Boulevard, its orientation dividing the hills and flats, clarifies the territories of high and low, rich and poor, idle and industrious, fantasy and reality.

The bus is once again waiting. We hop, jump and skip one block up following Franklin east to the largest municipal recreation area in the nation. [45-53] Griffith Park is a wilderness preserve, a relief from crowds and congestion and the "lungs" for a polluted city. "Experts surmise (although little archeological work has been done in confirmation) that Gabrielino Indians lived and hunted in the Ferndell area."[14] In the early 19th century, a land grant was claimed by Corp. José Vicente Feliz, one of the original soldiers accompanying the forty-four pueblo settlers.[15] Subsequent owners were Antonio Coronel, Leon Baldwin, then in 1884, Griffith J. Griffith, who donated the land to the city twelve years later. After much doubt, giving scant budget for protection from sheepherders and Christmas tree predators, the city begrudgingly accepted. Sixteen years

Fig. 46

Fig. 47

Fig. 48

Fig. 49

Fig. 50

Fig. 51

Fig. 52

Fig. 53

Fig. 54

later, they flatly turned down the murderous Griffith's funding offers, but later accepted his will's trust for the construction of a planetarium and Greek Theater.[16] Also installed were hiking trails, bridal paths, pools, tennis courts, summer camps, trains, pony rides, golf courses, museums, a zoo and an educational compost facility.

Brown, green, dark, rugged and wild, crows caw, mosquitoes buzz, corrugated drains rust. Seventy year-old steps twist up breeze-blown ravines. Oak, sage, and pine give shade through summer heat waves and hold the soil through winter torrents. Near the zoo, peacocks call; up camp road, children shout. At night, coyotes howl over the freeway drone. There are stone retaining walls; burnt out tree trunks, painted steel reservoirs, high-intensity towers, dried out horse droppings, bark-carved initials, bumpy-back mountain ridges and hawks hovering against Glendale's smoggy skyline. In short, the nation's largest municipal park is unique not only for its size, but for its geological significance and staunch western character.

New York's Central Park, Philadelphia's Fairmount and San Francisco's Golden Gate are easily accessible. Griffith, unfortunately, is not.[17] Lacking sufficient connection with Los Angeles city proper, the car rather than the cyclist, equestrian or pedestrian, predominates. Touching many cities and districts, as with its cut-off older cousin the L.A. River[18] [54-57] perhaps one day the park's full potential to bind and benefit may be realized.

Fig. 55

Fig. 56

Fig. 57

Hiking up the twisting trails, we face north to Rancho Los Encinos, [58] the mission and the mountains beyond, then south to the towers, [59] the antique homes along South Park Front Walk, [60] and at the point, the old light house. Preparing to reenter the hustle-bustle, we board the bus and wind out onto Hillhurst along the Pueblo's original western boundary edge[19] until we reach shimmering MacArthur Park. [61]

Within sight of the score billion dollar Bunker Hill, these thirty-two acres bound by 6th, 8th, Park View and Alvarado, were offered, in the mid-nineteenth century for approximately eight dollars. A ravine filled with water and alkali cones, the terminus to two street car lines, Mayor William Workman, unable to sell, turned it into a lake.[20] By 1896, families could be seen boating, attending Sunday concerts, feeding ducks and running about its undulating shores. [62-67]

Later, as one of the city's original parks, Westlake (as MacArthur was originally called) was to be linked (together with Griffith, Exposition, Echo, Central, the Plaza, Elysian, Sycamore Grove, Eastlake and Hollenbeck) by a series of parkways in an urban plan that was not realized. Instead, in 1934, this lushly landscaped loch was lopped in two.[21]

Yet even so, surrounded by bungalow courts, apartment buildings, restaurants, stores, the Elks

Fig. 58

Fig. 59

Fig. 60

WEST COAST
WESTLAKE
THEATRE

Fig. 61

Fig. 62

Fig. 63

Fig. 64

Fig. 65

Fig. 66

Fig. 67

Club Building, Otis Parsons and Chouinard Art Institute, a mildly bohemian neighborhood evolved.

Ironically, then in 1952, Westlake was renamed as part of a William Randolph Hearst funded campaign to elect WWII General Douglas MacArthur president. Some thirty-five years later, it was drained and relandscaped. And now with soccer balls rolling, picnic ants marching, chess pieces moving and its own Metro station, it functions as a much needed amenity, homeless refuge, shelter and venue for permitted protest. [68]

From here, triumphant or resigned, we head down Alvarado to Venice Boulevard and trace the Red Car Balloon Route to the sea. Back then, West L.A. [69] was open fields--home to a fox, not yet Century City. Then abruptly, romantic period scenery was dismantled to make way for harsh futuristic reality.[22] [70-79]

At the end of the route, our balloon flown away, we step down onto Windward Circle--once the Grand Lagoon and Midway Plaisance--axis to the Boardwalk by the sea. Stretching from Santa Monica to Venice, Ocean Front Walk (a pedestrian, skate and bike path) is Southern California's most popular attraction. Whereas Universal City Walk is private property, Third Street Promenade and Glendon Avenue are controlled, the Boardwalk still retains a funky tradition. It was not

Fig. 68

Fig. 69

Fig. 70

Fig. 71

Fig. 72

Fig. 73

Fig. 74

Fig. 75

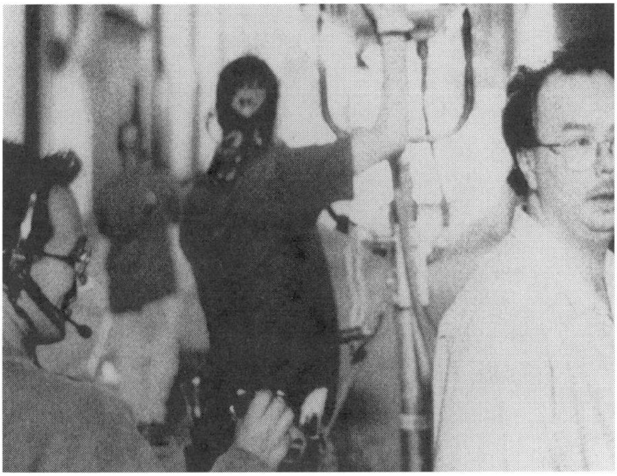

Fig. 76

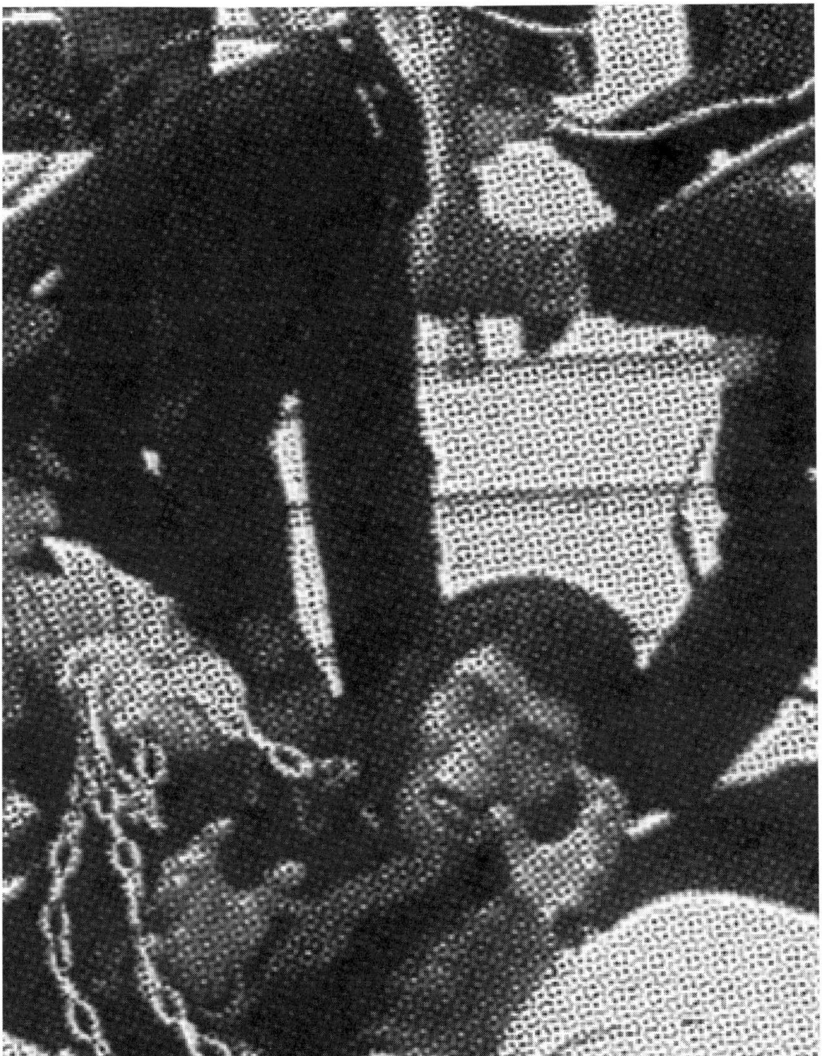

Fig. 77

Fig. 78

Fig. 79

repaved like Hollywood nor did it enjoy the constancy of Westwood. Instead, like the rollercoasters on its old piers, its popularity had ups and downs.

The Boardwalk began as part of Abbot Kinney's "Venice of America," a beach development of canals, residences, hotels and cultural buildings. [80-89] From 1904 through the thirties, it remained an active red car destination and tourist vacation grounds. In 1946 however, both the tidelands lease and the right to operate the Venice Pier were lost. The trolley stopped and as a result the theme parks began to close.

In the meantime, while Pacific Ocean Pier went belly up, coffeehouse bohemians and hotel hippies were mixing with the Oakwood African-American community and Jewish senior enclaves. The result: Boardwalk peddlers were replaced by Bongo drummers, Bubble Blowers, Ragtime Pianists, Jazz Flutists, Jugglers, Psychics, Fortune Tellers, Portrait Artists and multi-flavored clouds of incense. Meanwhile closer to the water, bare bathers enjoyed nature's touch 'til police presented pre-'84 Olympics tickets curtailing tanning.

Though hard-fought grass roots and anti-development struggles continue, now, between breaths of fresh air and tastes of salty concession, it is safe to say that consistent with its origins and architectural style, the Venice Renaissance has given millions an opportunity to let loose.

Fig. 80

WHITE
HOTEL AN
ANTLER

Fig. 81

HOTEL
WALDORF

Fig. 82

Fig. 83

Fig. 84

Fig. 85

Fig. 86

Fig. 87

Fig. 88

Fig. 89

Yes, let loose and why not? Is not rest essential...recovery, renewal, reflection? No more riding. With the sun setting, we sit back, sigh, take a sip and see out to sea...out past the ocean edge to new horizons as we dwell upon our day's tour. [90]

Oh Italian examples: canals, lagoons, a seaside path, a walled city, a central dome, ordered squares and a Medieval bridge. Oh beloved Central Library: a soft zone of transition amid modern mayhem and Beaux Arts distinction. Oh Temporary Contemporary: a catalyst for culture from a low-cost conversion kernel. Oh Hollywood Boulevard: a clarifying corridor, oversized development, humble preservation. Oh La Brea Pits: a landmark finally fenced, a museum overanxious to expand. Oh Griffith Park: an urban wilderness, an encroaching system. Oh MacArthur: a lake halved, a population several times doubled. Oh Westwood: a veteran village, colored concrete, gravestones, giant dice... Monopoly!?!

Oh child-filled plazas...oh City Beautiful past...oh shelved urban plans...oh monuments of broken china...oh fertile earth below...oh cloudless sky above...oh...oh...oh... ***Oh sleeping stone Categories of Knowledge...AWAKE!*** Connect our city's public space stars until Statecraft barometers indicate a civilization alive, vital, thriving. [91]

Urban organization out west...? It happened in Venice--there and here. Now, not only in distinguished Florence, but in disjointed L.A., is not civic Renaissance possible?

Fig. 90

OPHY

Fig. 91

***

1 "Bridging the gap between old and new, this oasis of populist pastime in the west downtown desert of high-investment exclusivity was originally filled with Olive trees and their biblical branches of peace." *Los Angeles-The City Observed* (New York: Vintage Books, 1984), pp. 18-20.

2 The new Bunker Hill skyline emulates Manhattan; the Music Center referring to Lincoln Center. Broadway's Beaux Arts office blocks emulated Chicago of the early 20th century.

3 See Leonard Pitt and Dale Pitt, *Los Angeles: A-Z* (Berkeley and Los Angeles, University of California Press, 1997) p. 383. By administrative admission, Los Angeles remains seriously deficient in all categories of parks and recreation areas. Adequate in acreage proportionally (due to enormous Griffith Park), parkland is otherwise scarce, especially at the neighborhood level. Encompassing parks, preserves, beaches and historic sites, our public spaces have been obtained by charitable donation, governmental acquisition, legal action and hard fought grass roots battles (for example, Plummer Park). National Parks include Angeles National Forest and the Santa Monica Mountains National Preserve. The State runs most heavily-used beaches, a large portion of the Santa Monica Mountains and historic sites such as Will Rogers State Park and Rancho Los Encinos State Park. The County maintains a large network of parks, recreation areas, natural areas and centers, wildlife and wildflower sanctuaries and golf courses. The county network was expanded in the 30s and by 1959, 140 parks comprised 11,400 acres with 10.5 miles of beaches. The city has 150 recreation centers and 350 parks with over 15,000 acres. With such variety, it is easy to confuse public with private or semi-private space. One test is the frequency of permitted public protest and demonstrations. What were the results of this test during the 2000 Democratic National Convention? [92-99]

Fig. 92

Fig. 93

Fig. 94

Fig. 95

4 Just two years after Westwood's design, he, together with the Olmstead Brothers, authored the report "Parks, Playgrounds and Beaches for the Los Angeles Region." Not only did this report warn of subdivision and development dangers, but it proposed an ambitious plan for improvement and linking the county's amenities.
5 These once indigenous rolling hills were taken from Native Americans to become Rancho San Jose de Buenos Ayres in 1840. Later, Maximo Alanis transferred ownership to the Wolfskill family. In 1922, the Janss corporation bought 3,300 acres bounded by the National Soldiers Home on the west, Los Angeles Country Club and Beverly Hills on the east, Pico on the south and the foothills on the north.
6 Westwood Village was drawn out as part of "a master plan that hinged on a decision to donate a large portion of the property for a U.C. campus." See Leonard Pitt and Dale Pitt, *Los Angeles: A-Z* (Berkeley and Los Angeles, University of California Press, 1997) pp. 542-543. Laid out by Architect and Urban Planner Harland Bartholomew in 1928, the Janss Investment Company, "performed the extraordinary coup of offering...a small but highly developable site for UCLA. This ensured the inordinately high value of the surrounding Janss-owned real estate." See *Los Angeles-The City Observed* (New York: Vintage Books, 1984), p. 197.
7 In 1996, 24,000 undergrads, 11,000 grads. Andrea Schulte-Peevers and David Peevers, *Los Angeles* (Melbourne: Lonely Planet Publications, 1999) pg. 173.
8 *Los Angeles: A-Z* (Berkeley and Los Angeles, University of California Press, 1997) pp. 328. There were 100 stores by 1940. The area including the surrounding houses and apartments is now know as the Miracle Mile district.

9 The Pavilion for Japanese Art was originally designed for another location.

10 Oddly, this new identity is threatened by a proposal to level all LACMA buildings and replace them with the winning design of five entries. Though not all entries leveled the complex, all encroached further onto the park. One featured a freeway-like structure running through the grounds. Another was fronted with a large treeless plaza of which the Sheriff's Department would have enthusiastically approved. Even the most tasteful of the entries, perhaps to avoid being considered stale, added large bright-colored volumes to its roof. Funds for construction were sought through a misleading city "Museum Seismic Retrofit" measure which was voted down in 2002.

11 Leonard Pitt and Dale Pitt, *Los Angeles: A-Z* (Berkeley and Los Angeles, University of California Press, 1997) pp. 203.

12 Ibid. Also see Richard Longstreth, *City Center to Regional Mall-Architecture, the Automobile, and Retailing in Los Angeles* (Cambridge: The MIT Press) p. 85.

13 Ibid.

14 Leonard Pitt and Dale Pitt, *Los Angeles: A-Z* (Berkeley and Los Angeles, University of California Press, 1997) pp. 183-184.

15 Of these 44 settlers, two were Spanish; the remainder were of Mestizo blood--Indigenous, African. Weaver, John D. *El Pueblo Grande: Los Angeles from the Brush Huts of the Yangna to the Skyscrapers of the Modern Megalopolis.* Los Angeles: Private Press, 1973.

16 Imprisoned for attempting to murder his wife--who escaped by jumping out a Venice hotel window after having been shot through the eye by her drunken husband--Griffith, a secret alcoholic, was incarcerated a mere two years for the crime. See Hjelte, George, *Footprints in the Parks* (Los Angeles: Public Service Publications).

Fig. 96

Fig. 97

Fig. 98

FOR LEAS
UP TO 9000 SQFT · PARKING
COURTESY TO BROKER
213·746–2710
AUTO
PAWN

Fig. 99

17 See David Gebhard and Robert Winter, *Los Angeles-An Architectural Guide* (Salt Lake City: Gibbs-Smith Publishers, 1994) pp. 167-168.

18 Millions of years older than the adjacent mountains, the Los Angeles River is a rare antecedent stream, one of but a handful worldwide. Despite this relationship the 5 Freeway separated it from the park forcing equestrians to first ford a flood control channel then go through a tunnel under a state freeway.

19 Douglas R. Suisman, *Los Angeles Boulevard: Eight X-Rays of the Body Public* (Los Angeles: Los Angeles Forum for Architecture and Urban Design, 1989) pp. 12-15.

20 Charles Moore, Peter Becker and Regula Cambell, *Los Angeles: A-Z* (Berkeley and Los Angeles, University of California Press, 1997) p. 311.

21 Greg Hise and William Deverell, *Eden by Design-The 1930 Olmsted-Bartholomew Plan for the Los Angeles Region* (Berkeley and Los Angeles: University of California Press, 2000) pp.24-28. Part of a hierarchy with roots in Los Angeles' City Beautiful past, the playground was for everyday recreation; the local park, for community events and relations; and large preserves for excursions, camping and sleep-overs. The Olmsteads, Barthlomew, Methodist minister Dana Bartlett and many others contributed to this progressive movement.

22 For a description of the Balloon Route, see Norman Klein, 20th Century Los Angeles-Power, Promotion and Social Conflict. For Century City see, *Los Angeles: A-Z* (Berkeley and Los Angeles, University of California Press, 1997) pp. 82-83. "In Conquest of the Planet of the Apes (1972), Century City represented a metropolis of the future..." Two decades later, a union protest (Justice for Janitors) resulted in eerily reminiscent scenes. Location filming often takes over public space, rendering it temporarily useless, then confusing its public status with sensationalistic imagery.

Fig. 1

aeromexico
UNITED
VIAJE FELIZ
VENT
BOLETOS DE AVION
ANTES D
MPRAR CONSULTE NUEST
OS PRECIOS
COMPARE
GA... LLEGO Y ME LO
LEVO!!!

Fig. 2

Tubeless and Car-free

Ahhh, the neighborhood. Green lawns, white picket fences, shady tree-lined walks, little red wagons and grandma on the porch. Fount of childhood memories, venue of our life's first impressions: first kiss, first day of school, training wheels, playing house. Sentimentally, the neighborhood is the foundation of our life cycle and the source of our deepest, most sensitive emotions. A city stage upon which we enact our domestic lives, it is the home base of our urban existence. [1]

Yet when we look at a map of our city, we immediately confront snags in this mythic model. Our neighborhoods have funny shapes, jagged political boundaries. Their names often seem incongruous.[1] Near and far from downtown, hills, ocean, rivers, mountains; divided, of varied age, amenity and political power; these districts and residential zones bear token remnants of our traditional view. [2-11]

Fig. 3

Fig. 4

Fig. 5

Fig. 6

Fig. 7

Fig. 8

Fig. 9

Fig. 10

Fig. 11

Our changing neighborhoods have been the subject of many studies. In one, maps drawn by average residents in South Los Angeles, Westwood, Fairfax, Boyle Heights and Northridge revealed striking perceptions.[2] Boyle Heights was compact, limited to a few blocks. Northridge was expansive, reaching out to the ocean and beyond the edges of the county. What does this extreme contrast reflect? [12-13]

Boyle Heights, one of Los Angeles' first suburbs, emerged in the 1880s connected to downtown by streetcar. With short regular blocks, a retail corridor along Brooklyn Avenue and easy access to community buildings, it was populated by artisans, investors, white collar Yankees and Spanish surnamed families.[3] The population shifted and by the 1920s, the area consisted more of Jews, Mexicans, Japanese, African-Americans and Russians. Temples, churches, libraries, social centers, schools, hospitals, public baths, cemeteries and other public resources were added. Then, in the 50s, trolley lines were illegally removed and construction of freeways begun.[4] Eventually the 101 Santa Ana, 5 Golden State, 10 San Bernardino and 60 Pomona would tear through this nineteenth century grid, uprooting homes, dead-ending streets, dividing communities, interrupting foot traffic, separating families and friends and in one brutal instance, lopping off the southern half of a hundred-year-old English style lake park. [14-24]

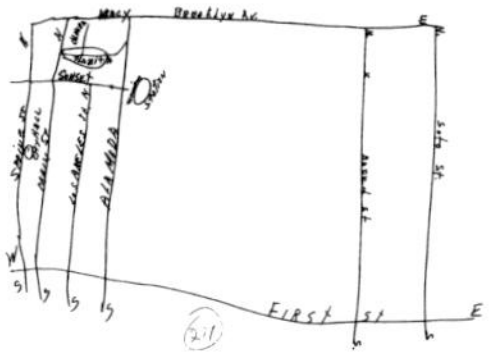

11A. ACTUAL CITIZEN'S MAP - BOYLE HEIGHTS

Fig. 12

11B. COMPOSITE CITIZEN IMAGE - BOYLE HEIGHTS

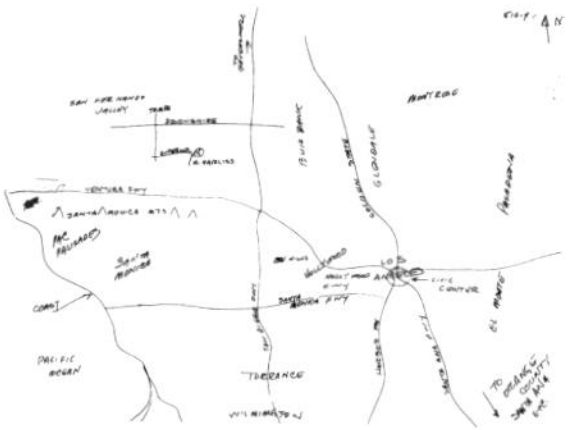

8A. ACTUAL CITIZEN'S MAP - NORTHRIDGE

Fig. 13

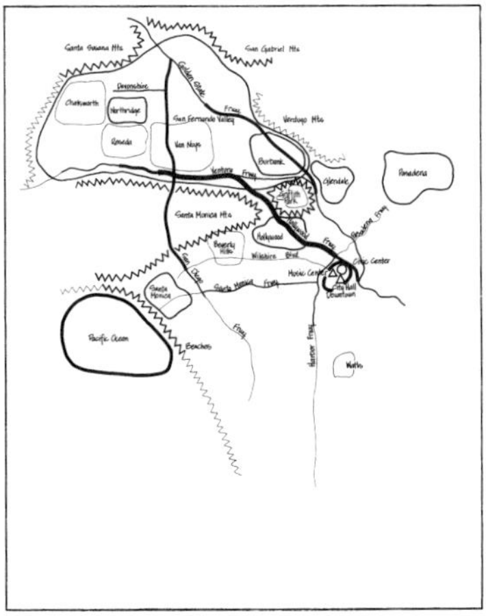

8B. COMPOSITE CITIZEN IMAGE - NORTHRIDGE

Fig. 14

Fig. 15

Fig. 16

Fig. 17

Fig. 18

Fig. 19

Fig. 20

HOLLENBECK LAKE
BRIDGE 453-1359

Fig. 21

Fig. 22

Now, Boyle Heights is predominately Mexican and Central American. Signs have changed, some new buildings have appeared. Stores and institutions have been remodeled. Along Cesar Chavez (formerly Brooklyn) are White Memorial Hospital, an LAFD station, murals, restaurants, businesses and shops. Along First Street are Mariachi Plaza, the Post Office, the Hollenbeck Youth Center, the Community Service Organization, the Ben Franklin library, low-income housing complexes and Evergreen Cemetery. The churches, parks, schools and houses are generally early twentieth century and for the most part, well-maintained.[5]

While Boyle Heights was dissected by freeways, Northridge was formed by them. Once part of Benjamin F. Porter's ranch, this "watering place in the desert" became in 1908 a railway stop and by the 30's, the "horse capital of the valley." First called Zelzah, then North Los Angeles, it was later renamed after *Northridge Farms* the venue for an annual equestrian event. In 1956, a 350-acre college campus replaced an orange grove off Nordhoff Boulevard. And soon after, the rural surroundings area were subdivided into single family tracts. Three freeways—the 405 to the east, the 101 to the south and the 118 to the north—serve, but do not run through this mainly middle and upper-class district. In 1994, it was the epicenter of a 6.7 earthquake. Estimated damage ran as high as twenty billion dollars yet the area has recovered quickly.[6]

While Boyle Heights remains for the large part pedestrian, it has lost luster to the drone, pollution and sheer mass of the freeways. Quaint hundred-year-old cottages are impotent to convey their charm next to thirty-foot high concrete barriers. These state-maintained dividers ruin the natural landscape, destroy community coherence and spread a prevailing heaviness.

Over the hill in Northridge the freeways elongated the neighborhood. The streets were widened; the use of the car, emphasized. Drivers hop into oversized vehicles to retrieve even minor items such as cigarettes or soda. Malls such as Northridge Plaza and University Center hold hundreds (sometimes thousands) of parking places. Soccer clubs bring extra balls in case one is kicked into the street. Housing tracts stretch along freeway arteries, in some places eight lanes wide. [25] Devonshire Boulevard's intersection with (the even wider) Sepulveda is injurious, the opposite of a plaza: an anti-center, void not vital, a no-man's land. [26] Children no longer ask their mothers if they can play across the street. Instead, driven inside, they are sealed off, pacified, indoctrinated.

Fig. 23

Fig. 24

A late eighteenth century inner-city streetcar district and a mid-twentieth century valley freeway suburb are ironically now both ordered by the auto. Not only have cars detached individuals from their neighborhood collective, they have weakened communication skills and severed relations between residents, small businesses and local institutions. Studies show residents are less aware of their neighborhood's features, its resources, its natural landscape. Delicate bonds are broken and even self-identity becomes redirected away from where you live and on to what you drive. The car becomes the connection between work and home with many residents rarely stepping foot onto the sidewalk. Traditionally, streets serve the dual purpose of movement and exchange (social, cultural, economic). Car traffic has eroded that duality and physically taken over previously collective territory.[7] [27-29]

One study showing how traffic severely erodes territory asked residents to mark off what parts of their immediate surroundings they considered theirs. Residents of lightly trafficked streets marked off the entire street and sidewalk. They had three times as many friends and twice as many acquaintances. Those of heavily trafficked streets timidly marked off their own front steps. Neither the street nor the sidewalk was

Fig. 25

Fig. 26

even collectively theirs. [27-29] There were less people gardening and less on their front porch. Residents abandoned their front rooms using them instead as buffers. Some moved altogether, increasing transience and alienation while eroding long term relationships.[8]

But autos are not the only undermining force. The wide and hostile raceways running through our neighborhoods force us inside to television. And does television then encourage a reclaiming of territory? Just the opposite, it purposely reinforces the loss by pacifying and further detaching viewers. TV undermines the neighborhood by promoting violence. Today 98% of US households have at least one television[9] and the average child watches on that television 8,000 murders before finishing elementary school. By age eighteen, the average American has seen 200,000 acts of violence including 16,000 murders.[10]

Television, although an audio/visual medium, *physically* moves people away from collective aspects of the neighborhood, [30-31] circumventing the traditional use of the porch and front yard as a zone of transition. The substitute transition to the collective then is, instead, a barrage of consumeristic messages, manipulative stories and overdone news reports. Children are robbed of their most essential occupation.

Fig. 27

Fig. 28

Fig. 29

Fig. 30

"The most common sacrifice to television is play—unorganized, unstructured, using-your-imagination play...the true and magical stuff of childhood."[11] [32] This loss cheats youth of a key part of their own childhood, of valuable opportunities to interact with other kids and adults, and of the ability to entertain themselves.[12] Television promotes inactivity: ". . .the cynicism and concern that many Americans voice involves the indifference of people who spend more time watching television than working with their neighbors."[13] Television is "a medium which presents information in a form that renders it simplistic, nonsubstantive, nonhistorical and non contextual."[14] Television reinforces both the detachment and loss of communication created by cars. It also promote alcoholism[15] and overconsumption, isolates us from nature and creates the "Mean World Syndrome."[16] [33]

In program after program, film after film, like a wrestling tag team, the colluding forces of television and the auto frame neighborhoods in car/TV terms. East Los Angeles: drive-bys and customized Chevys. The Westside: Mercedes moguls in the midst of mobile meetings. The Valley: Chrysler convertible consummations overlooking congested commuters. In Inglewood, civic leaders publically objected to this type of misrepresentation. The opening

Fig. 31

Fig. 32

sequence of the 1991 film *Grand Canyon* depicts a middle-aged executive whose car breaks down and is approached by African-American youth. Ominous music plays. A T-shirt is lifted; underneath, a gun. Then just in the nick of time, a tow-truck driver arrives, the frightening hum disappears and a choir sings.[17] The messages are clearly packaged and efficiently presented: unknown neighborhoods are dangerous; cars are protective.[18] Strategically scattered props such as stripped sedans and profuse graffiti rendered Inglewood--in reality a diverse middle-class town--as a crime-ridden ghetto.

Media manipulation is of course nothing new. Representing leadership, commitment, and determination, Hollywood neighborhood heroes are fearless, unflappable, thematically central and physically fitting in. *Bullet* was as light and well-groomed as his Victorian San Franciscan hillside home. *Shaft*, in his black overcoat was as tall and dark as the Manhattan skyscrapers among which he ambled. *Rocky*, in heels, leather short jacket and flattened fedora, was as squat and solid as a Philadelphia Brownstone.

A loan shark's thug, Rocky, to car-addicted Southern Californians, seemed out of place--an anachronism resembling the pedestrian tenement characters of playwright Sidney Kingsley's *Dead End*. Nonetheless, Rocky was

Fig. 33

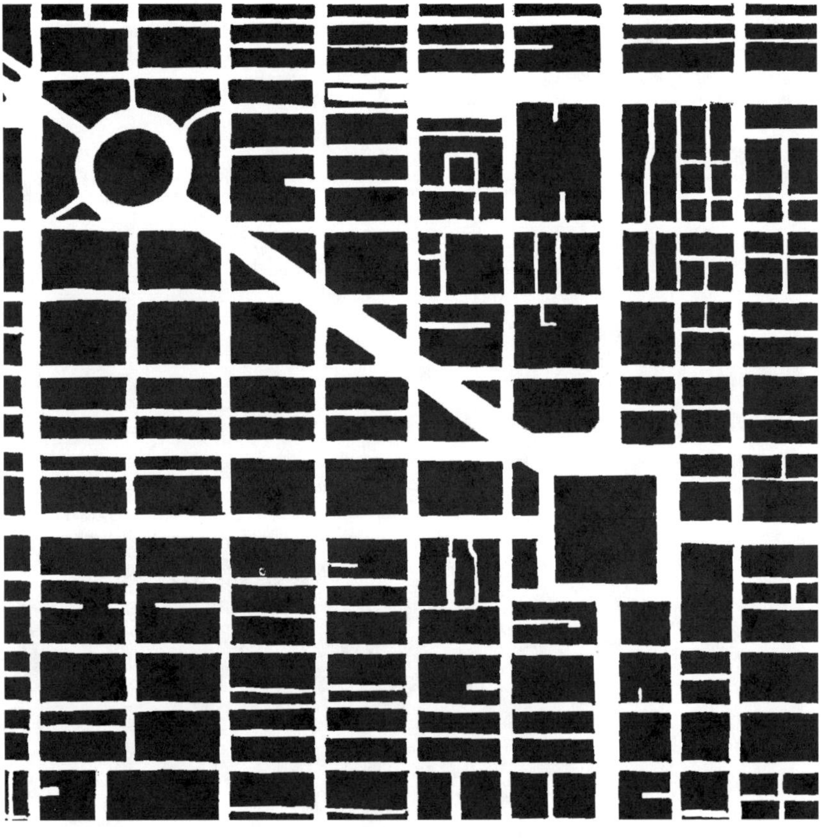

Fig. 34

humorously seductive. Unlike his chauffeured, organized-crime employer, he walks! As the story unfolds though, his car-lessness is used to define him as a bum, a nobody. Whereas the gangster villain in Dead End returns home, Rocky the bespectacled debt collector, has never left. Dead End concludes hopefully with the neighborhood's shaky order surviving a villainous visit. In Rocky, it is the system's cynical nature that endows the Italian Stallion (who walks teen-age girls home and carries drunks to shelter) with unbelievable opportunity. Though adolescents disobey him, adults insult him, the gym owner confiscates his locker, and his apartment "STINKS," animals like him, street vendors throw him fruit, he finds love and in the end, cutting across the city grid [34], ascends to hometown herohood bringing beer imbibing fight fans together for a frenzied celebratory barside broadcast. Strangely though, in the end, the Philadelphia neighborhood is revealed to be a red herring.[19] Its fate important? Unimportant. In fact, absent--the streetcorner singers, the front steps youth, the Brownstones--abandoned.

And with the neighborhood abandoned, have we become the "overfed" circus "clowns" in what James Howard Kunstler calls a "hostile cartoon environment," [35-37] or, are we merely the powerless *Peanuts* of Charles Shultz's imaginative pen? In that very popular comic, adult-like children roam through a world void of parents, principals, politicians, (architects, engineers) and planners. In one animated episode, Linus holds a pagan-like faith in a pumpkin patch. On Halloween, he goes against social order, patiently awaiting the "Great Pumpkin," recruiting another child to help his hopes. Ridiculing, the others leave for "tricks or treats," Charlie Brown receiving instead of candy, rocks from unseen, silent and disappointing adults.[20] Meanwhile, Charlie's dog, acting out a war fantasy of aerial assault is shot-down, crashing, then later rejoining the other characters in an imaginary abandoned French farm house—the Halloween Party. After festivities, the children again pass the patch. Linus is once again ridiculed and when his recruit turns against him, he is alone. Finally at dawn, he is led back to his somber room with its globe, gray walls, books leaning on the shelf, blue bed and red pillow.

Though Linus the protagonist is returned to the status quo, Snoopy is indifferent to it. Dressed as the WWI Flying Ace, alternately laughing and weeping as the toy piano tinkled from ballad to march (symbolizing the ambiva-

Fig. 35

Fig.36

Fig. 37

Fig. 38

lence of elders pining for their warm intimate past, then recklessly marching lockstep into Progress), he stole the show. Single-handedly parodying pilots and professionals, home-owners and hobbyists, small time writers and big time sportsmen, he was still but a beagle, unable to talk with people, angrily kicking at his owner's door when his bowl remained too long unfilled. Manufactured as pins, posters, and dolls, he accompanied children to bed—a distraction, a friend, an aid to understanding suburban contradictions. [38-49]

But communites are not cartoons. They are, as Norman Klein writes, more like "necklaces." And once "the clasp is removed, the necklace is as good as lost," replaced instead by an Auto/TV tag-team full-nelson.

So, hanging onto the remaining strings, what if, for but a moment, *we* confront contradictions. What if we turn off the ignition and remote control and try to imagine a pumpkin patch, not rejected, but tended, harvested, embraced. And homes full of hope and heroes of both genders. And all this not on a screen or the other side of our country, but here in this city, perhaps just down your street.

Beside the Franklin Hills, a short walk from Hollywood's east end, on Russell Avenue in the Los Feliz district, a California bungalow fitted

Fig. 39

Fig. 40

Fig. 41

Fig. 42

Fig. 43

Fig. 44

Fig. 45

Fig. 46

Fig. 47

Fig. 48

Fig. 49

Fig. 50

Fig. 51

Fig. 52

Fig. 53

with solar panels houses an entire organization. A drought-tolerant garden in front provides meditative transition to the street. In back, food is raised. Inside, the house is unpretentious, harkening back to the Craftsman heritage. [54-57]

Eco-Home founder Julia Russell uses streets for bicycling, sidewalks for walking and meeting neighbors as she relishes her car-free existence. Like a refreshing breeze, her influence has already led to the xeriscape conversion of many a front yard while thousands have toured and learned from her unique home. No broken windows, violent threats, suped up Mustangs, shifted grids, exposed wood studs, painted re-bar or wire glass, just quiet persistence in the face of local and legal challenge, rapidly changing populations, vandals, theft and traffic.

According to Julia, the "Eco" (from the Greek *oikos* meaning household) is the basic unit of the neighborhood and where care for the environment can begin. Russell consumes but a fraction of normal water volume. She reduces air pollution through the use of solar power for electricity and water heating. She uses non-toxic paints, finishes, furnishings, cleaning and hygienic products; composts her green waste; recycles aluminum, paper and plastic and pours gray water on thirsty plants. Her backyard organic orchard and vegetable garden supple-

Fig. 54

Fig. 55

Fig. 56

Fig. 57

ments her diet. And meanwhile she reaches out to not just a string, but a whole network, through mailings, meetings and a member's newsletter. One receptive member in nearby Sun Valley is Ellen Mackey.

On Mackey's typically residential street sit an eclectic mix of houses. Myrtle trees line the sidewalks.[21] [58] Surprisingly at the end of this ordinary cul-de-sac, [59-61] a tract home has been transformed--not into a colonial homestead, a plantation or a tudor mansion, but instead, a low-impact, resource-conserving humble ecohome. Gray water is siphoned out to the garden. Compost is rotated. Solar panels reduce grid energy requirements. Marigolds (not pesticides) repel insects from growing vegetables. Reflective ribbons distract hungry birds. Solar tubes bring light deep into the kitchen. The fruitful backyard, lush with fruit trees, bean vines and corn stalks is pleasantly detached while the front yard is a showcase of native plants. [62-65]

Another organization, just off of Vermont and First, back in Mid-City, is Eco-Village. Formed in the early 90s with the purpose of creating a residential enclave as the nucleus for reducing environmental impacts and raising the quality of life, it now has approximately 50 Eco-Villagers who reside with neighbors and other

Fig. 58

Fig. 59

Fig. 60

Fig. 61

Fig. 62

Fig. 63

Fig. 64

Fig. 65

Fig. 66

residents in over 60 units within a two block area. There are six organic gardens, 60 fruit trees, a composting center, consensus meetings, weekly vegetarian potlucks, a village newsletter and a special solar-powered unit. There is a discount to residents who remain car-free and a bicycle repair shop for the high percentage of transit-focused tenants. [66-68]

Strolling the sidewalk outside our own abodes, with cars hissing by and canned cackles, cries and characters casting a corrosive pall upon us, suddenly we come to our senses. Sentimental as we may be, no, the neighborhood is not mythic. Autos have driven us inward; TV tells us we must drive. And through all this, time and nature flow on. The seedling orange tree now towers with ant and milkfly covered fruit. The weeds grow through cracks in the once new step stones. The baby lizard is now full-grown catching a water bug in its jaws, waiting, then swallowing it live. Even on the tube, Captain Kangaroo has long since retired and the used car cowboy can no longer stand on his head. As we all age and our planet reacts to increased contamination, we stop and wonder. Can we begin to break free, joining Julia, Ellen, the Eco-Villagers and millions of other activists, preservationists, environmentalists and just plain good neighbors from downtown's Dome Village to Brazil's Curtiba to Gaviotas in the

Fig. 67

Columbian Llanos--caring for our environment, planting trees, unchaining our streets, ourselves, confronting the challenges of creating and maintaining healthy, self-sustaining communities both in the inner-city and outlying suburbs?

***

1 Often of Spanish or Indian origin, neighborhood names often seem out of place in their sterile high modern settings. Exaggerated picturesque illusions such as Shadow Hills, Lake View Terrace, Windsor Square or Realtor family names like Van Nuys, Leimert, Sawtelle seem to have little relevance to current appearance or population as well.

2 Lynch, Kevin, The Visual Environment of Los Angeles, Los Angeles Department of City Planning, 1971.

3 Along Echandia Street Leonard Pitt and Dale Pitt, *Los Angeles: A-Z* (Berkeley and Los Angeles, University of California Press, 1997), p. 56.

4 Both authors Michael Parenti and James Howard Kunstler have reported on this corporate conspiracy. See James Howard Kunstler, *The Geography of Nowhere* (New York: Simon and Schuster, 1993), pp. 91-92.

5 An inventory of historically significant sites was conducted prior to the planned installation of the eastbound Red Line. The number of these sites that will be preserved is anyone's guess.

6 Barbara Stanwick's horse breeding ranch designed by well-known African-American architect Paul Williams.

Leonard Pitt and Dale Pitt, *Los Angeles: A-Z* (Berkeley and Los Angeles, University of California Press, 1997), pp. 361

7 "Cars Steal Our Home Territory...And Inhibits Social Exchange" David Engwicht, Car Busters, No. 10, Winter 2000, p. 9.
8 Ibid., p. 8. The study was conducted by Donald Appleyard in San Francisco, 1970.
9 Breaking Free of TV (Washington, DC, TV Turnoff Network, 2000), p. 36.
10 Physicians Guide to Media Violence, American Medical Association
11 Leonard Jason and Libby Kennedy Hanaway, *Remote Control: A Sensible Approach to Kids, TV and the New Electronic Media.*
12 Breaking Free of TV (Washington, DC, TV Turnoff Network, 2000), p. 32.
13 A Nation of Spectators, The Report of the National Commission on Civic Renewal.
14 Neil Postman, *Amusing Ourselves to Death* (Penguin Books).
15 Breaking Free of TV (Washington, DC, TV Turnoff Network, 2000), p. 27. This study was particularly well documented.
16 Breaking Free of TV (Washington, DC, TV Turnoff Network, 2000), p. 26. Coined by Dr. George Gerber of the Annenberg School of Communication.
17 This civic and racial smear is then further fouled by a Hollywood favorite—individual heroics predominates over collective action. Strategically including a black hero, the story remains merely another rendition of what Michael Parenti describes as the "Paradigm of the Wagon Train vs. the Swarthy Hordes" Michael Parenti, "Rambo vs. the Swarthy Hordes," FAIR & KPFK, People's Video/Audio Tape No. 9.

Fig. 68

18 Just a few of the many negative messages conveyed by this main stream film include: leaving a major Boulevard is hazardous, if you do, neither pedestrians nor small business owners will help; youths are a threat (impossibly belligerent); problems in the African-American community are out of control, cyclical, compounded by the impotence of elders.

19 Or perhaps more accurately, the bait. With its colorful characters, rhythmic rows of steps, repetitive brick buildings, typical street side shops, old fashioned gym and waterfront docks, viewers were caught hook, line and sinker. Map of Philadelphia by Allan B. Jacobs, *Great Streets* (Cambridge: MIT Press, 1995) p. 236.

20 The F-16 engineer, the missile coating chemist, the oil company geologist...

21 The bases of these biblical trees, as if having given up on stylistic miracles, seep over onto the sidewalk, seemingly trying to escape.